Depositions and Discovery

The Practice Commentaries Series

Depositions and Discovery
Rules and Commentaries

2003/2004 Edition

Linda G. Birchall
Powell, Goldstein, Frazer & Murphy

Arnold Klein
Meltzer, Lippe, Goldstein & Schlissel

Janis M. Meyer
Dewey Ballantine

Shane Read
U.S. Attorney's Office, Nothern District of Texas

Mark D. Risk
D'Agostino, Levine & Landesman

Professor David A. Sonenshein
Temple University Beasley School of Law

G. Leroy Street
The Street Law Firm

The National Institute for Trial Advocacy

© 2003 by the National Institute for Trial Advocacy

PRINTED IN THE UNITED STATES OF AMERICA.
ALL RIGHTS RESERVED.

Depositions and Discovery: Rules and Commentaries, 2003/2004 Edition (NITA, 2003)

ISBN 1-55681-847-5

Table of Contents

Preface

Depositions and Discovery is another pamphlet in the NITA Practice Commentaries series. These publications are designed to present a brief and focused review of the basic issues and practice concepts surrounding deposition and discovery, particularly Part V. Depositions and Discovery of the Federal Rules of Civil Procedure, Rules 26 through 37. In addition, Rule 45. Subpoena and its commentary are included because of the central importance of the rule in achieving the goals of discovery. Finally, we have included commentaries on 28 USC §§ 1781, 1782, and 1783 and the statutes themselves—which deal with the process of gathering information at the request of non-U.S. judicial authorities and obtaining information in foreign jurisdictions.

These commentaries are, with some modification, derived from the earlier NITA publication *Practice Commentaries—FRCP*, and like that book the FRCP rules precede the commentaries.

This series of publications is designed to be used by both practicing attorneys and law students. The focused material permits one to quickly and conveniently review the rules and the practice issues. For students it provides a framework in which to identify possible issues and basic concepts of depositions and discovery.

As with any source, the commentaries are not intended to be a detailed review of all the issues but to provide practical observations and excellent starting points for using and understanding the deposition and discovery rules.

Acknowledgments

Depositions and Discovery and the Practice Commentaries Project series owe their existences to the many professionals who are a part of the National Institute for Trial Advocacy. This series is unique in that these practice-oriented commentaries were first written for electronic distribution through Lexis.

First I want to thank our Editorial Board for the high editorial standards they have set for this project. Shelly Goethals, Manager, Administrative Operations, makes sure those editorial standards are met and the books are produced; Frank Alan, Editor Electronic Publishing, is the contact point for the commentary authors and consistently performs at an exemplary level; and Jude Phillips, NITA's Graphics Specialist, brought a creative touch to the composition of the material.

Most of all I want to thank the authors—Professor David A. Sonenshein, Linda G. Birchall, Shane Read, Arnold Klein, G. Leroy Street, Mark D. Risk, and Janis M. Meyer—all of whom so generously shared their practice expertise.

Anthony Bocchino
Editor-in-Chief
The National Institute for Trial Advocacy

Federal Rules of Civil Procedure
V. Depositions and Discovery

Rule 26. General Provisions Governing Discovery; Duty of Disclosure

(a) Required Disclosures; Methods to Discover Additional Matter.

(1) Initial Disclosures. Except in categories of proceedings specified in Rule 26(a)(1)(E), or to the extent otherwise stipulated or directed by order, a party must, without awaiting a discovery request, provide to other parties:

(A) the name and, if known, the address and telephone number of each individual likely to have discoverable information that the disclosing party may use to support its claims or defenses, unless solely for impeachment, identifying the subjects of the information;

(B) a copy of, or a description by category and location of, all documents, data compilations, and tangible things that are in the possession, custody, or control of the party and that the disclosing party may use to support its claims or defenses, unless solely for impeachment;

(C) a computation of any category of damages claimed by the disclosing party, making available for inspection and copying as under Rule 34 the documents or other evidentiary material, not privileged or protected from disclosure, on which such computation is based, including materials bearing on the nature and extent of injuries suffered; and

(D) for inspection and copying as under Rule 34 any insurance agreement under which any person carrying on an insurance business may be liable to satisfy part or all of a judgment which may be entered in the action or to indemnify or reimburse for payments made to satisfy the judgment.

(E) The following categories of proceedings are exempt from initial disclosure under Rule 26(a)(1):

(i) an action for review on an administrative record;

(ii) a petition for habeas corpus or other proceeding to challenge a criminal conviction or sentence;

(iii) an action brought without counsel by a person in custody of the United States, a state, or as state subdivision;

(iv) an action to enforce or quash an administrative summons or subpoena;

(v) an action by the United States to recover benefit payments;

(vi) an action by the United States to collect on a student loan guaranteed by the United States;

(vii) a proceeding ancillary to proceedings in other courts; and

(viii) an action to enforce an arbitration award.

These disclosures must be made at or within 14 days after the Rule 26(f) conference unless a different time is set by stipulation or court order, or unless a party objects during the conference that initial disclosures are not appropriate in the circumstances of the action and states the objection in the Rule 26(f) discovery plan. In ruling on the objection, the court must determine what disclosures—if any—are to be made, and set the time for disclosure. Any party first served or otherwise joined after the Rule 26(f) conference must make these disclosures within 30 days after being served or joined unless a different time is set by stipulation or court order. A party must make its initial disclosures based on the information then reasonably available to it and is not excused from making its disclosures because it has not fully completed its investigation of the case or because it challenges the sufficiency of another party's disclosures or because another party has not made its disclosures.

(2) Disclosure of Expert Testimony.

(A) In addition to the disclosures required by paragraph

RULE 26. GENERAL PROVISIONS GOVERNING DISCOVERY; DUTY OF DISCLOSURE

(1), a party shall disclose to other parties the identity of any person who may be used at trial to present evidence under Rules 702, 703, or 705 of the Federal Rules of Evidence.

(B) Except as otherwise stipulated or directed by the court, this disclosure shall, with respect to a witness who is retained or specially employed to provide expert testimony in the case or whose duties as an employee of the party regularly involve giving expert testimony, be accompanied by a written report prepared and signed by the witness. The report shall contain a complete statement of all opinions to be expressed and the basis and reasons therefor; the data or other information considered by the witness in forming the opinions; any exhibits to be used as a summary of or support for the opinions; the qualifications of the witness, including a list of all publications authored by the witness within the preceding ten years; the compensation to be paid for the study and testimony; and a listing of any other cases in which the witness has testified as an expert at trial or by deposition within the preceding four years.

(C) These disclosures shall be made at the times and in the sequence directed by the court. In the absence of other directions from the court or stipulation by the parties, the disclosures shall be made at least 90 days before the trial date or the date the case is to be ready for trial or, if the evidence is intended solely to contradict or rebut evidence on the same subject matter identified by another party under paragraph (2)(B), within 30 days after the disclosure made by the other party. The parties shall supplement these disclosures when required under subdivision (e)(1).

(3) Pretrial Disclosures. In addition to the disclosures required by Rule 26(a)(1) and (2), a party must provide to other parties and promptly file with the court the following information regarding the evidence that it may present at trial other than solely for impeachment:

(A) the name and, if not previously provided, the address and telephone number of each witness, separately identifying those whom the party expects to present and those whom the party may call if the need arises;

(B) the designation of those witnesses whose testimony is expected to be presented by means of a deposition and, if not taken stenographically, a transcript of the pertinent portions of the deposition testimony; and

(C) an appropriate identification of each document or other exhibit, including summaries of other evidence, separately identifying those which the party expects to offer and those which the party may offer if the need arises.

Unless otherwise directed by the court, these disclosures must be made at least 30 days before trial. Within 14 days thereafter, unless a different time is specified by the court, a party may serve and promptly file a list disclosing (i) any objections to the use under Rule 32(a) of a deposition designated by another party under Rule 26(a)(3)(B), and (ii) any objection, together with the grounds therefor, that may be made to the admissibility of materials identified under Rule 26(a)(3)(C). Objections not so disclosed, other than objections under Rules 402 and 403 of the Federal Rules of Evidence, are waived unless excused by the court for good cause.

(4) Form of Disclosures. Unless the court orders otherwise, all disclosures under Rules 26(a)(1) through (3) must be made in writing, signed, and served.

(5) Methods to Discover Additional Matter. Parties may obtain discovery by one or more of the following methods: depositions upon oral examination or written questions; written interrogatories; production of documents or things or permission to enter upon land or other property under Rule 34 or 45(a)(1)(C), for inspection and other purposes; physical and mental examinations; and requests for admission.

(b) Discovery Scope and Limits. Unless otherwise limited by order of the court in accordance with these rules, the scope of discovery is as follows:

RULE 26. GENERAL PROVISIONS GOVERNING DISCOVERY; DUTY OF DISCLOSURE

(1) In General. Parties may obtain discovery regarding any matter, not privileged, that is relevant to the claim or defense of any party, including the existence, description, nature, custody, condition, and location of any books, documents, or other tangible things and the identity and location of persons having knowledge of any discoverable matter. For good cause, the court may order discovery of any matter relevant to the subject matter involved in the action. Relevant information need not be admissible at the trial if the discovery appears reasonably calculated to lead to the discovery of admissible evidence. All discovery is subject to the limitations imposed by Rule 26(b)(2)(i), (ii), and (iii).

(2) Limitations. By order, the court may alter the limits in these rules on the number of depositions and interrogatories or the length of depositions under Rule 30. By order or local rule, the court may also limit the number of requests under Rule 36. The frequency or extent of use of the discovery methods otherwise permitted under these rules and by any local rule shall be limited by the court if it determines that: (i) the discovery sought is unreasonably cumulative or duplicative, or is obtainable from some other source that is more convenient, less burdensome, or less expensive; (ii) the party seeking discovery has had ample opportunity by discovery in the action to obtain the information sought; or (iii) the burden or expense of the proposed discovery outweighs its likely benefit, taking into account the needs of the case, the amount in controversy, the parties' resources, the importance of the issues at stake in the litigation, and the importance of the proposed discovery in resolving the issues. The court may act upon its own initiative after reasonable notice or pursuant to a motion under Rule 26(c).

(3) Trial Preparation: Materials. Subject to the provisions of subdivision (b)(4) of this rule, a party may obtain discovery of documents and tangible things otherwise discover- able under subdivision (b)(1) of this rule and prepared in anticipation of litigation or for trial by or for another party or by or for that other party's representative (including the other party's attorney, consultant, surety, indemnitor, insurer, or agent) only upon a showing that the party seeking discovery has substantial need of the materials in the preparation of the party's case and that the party is unable without undue hardship to obtain the substantial equivalent of the materials by other means. In ordering discovery of such materials when the required showing has been made, the court shall protect against disclosure of the mental impressions, conclusions, opinions, or legal theories of an attorney or other representative of a party concerning the litigation.

A party may obtain without the required showing a statement concerning the action or its subject matter previously made by that party. Upon request, a person not a party may obtain without the required showing a statement concerning the action or its subject matter previously made by that person. If the request is refused, the person may move for a court order. The provisions of Rule 37(a)(4) apply to the award of expenses incurred in relation to the motion. For purposes of this paragraph, a statement previously made is (A) a written statement signed or otherwise adopted or approved by the person making it, or (B) a stenographic, mechanical, electrical, or other recording, or a transcription thereof, which is a substantially verbatim recital of an oral statement by the person making it and contemporaneously recorded.

(4) Trial Preparation: Experts.

(A) A party may depose any person who has been identified as an expert whose opinions may be presented at trial. If a report from the expert is required under subdivision (a)(2)(B), the deposition shall not be conducted until after the report is provided.

(B) A party may, through interrogatories or by deposition, discover facts known or opinions held by an expert who has been retained or specially employed by another party in anticipation of litigation or preparation for trial and who is not expected to be called as a witness at trial, only as provided in Rule 35(b) or upon a showing of exceptional circumstances under which it is impracticable for the party seeking discovery to obtain facts or opinions on the same subject by other means.

(C) Unless manifest injustice would result, (i) the court shall require that the party seeking discovery pay the expert a reasonable fee for time spent in responding to discovery under this subdivision; and (ii) with respect to discovery obtained under subdivision (b)(4)(B) of this rule the court shall require the party seeking discovery to pay the other party a fair portion of the fees and expenses reasonably incurred by the latter party in obtaining facts and opinions from the expert.

(5) Claims of Privilege or Protection of Trial Preparation Materials. When a party withholds information otherwise discoverable under these rules by claiming that it is privileged or subject to protection as trial preparation material, the party shall make the claim expressly and shall describe the nature of the documents, communications, or things not produced or disclosed in a manner that, without revealing information itself privileged or protected, will enable other parties to assess the applicability of the privilege or protection.

(c) Protective Orders. Upon motion by a party or by the person from whom discovery is sought, accompanied by a certification that the movant has in good faith conferred or attempted to confer with other affected parties in an effort to resolve the dispute without court action, and for good cause shown, the court in which the action is pending or alternatively, on matters relating to a deposition, the court in the district where the deposition is to be taken may make any order which justice requires to protect a party or person from annoyance, embarrassment, oppression, or undue burden or expense, including one or more of the following:

(1) that the disclosure or discovery not be had;

(2) that the disclosure or discovery may be had only on specified terms and conditions, including a designation of the time or place;

(3) that the discovery may be had only by a method of discovery other than that selected by the party seeking discovery;

(4) that certain matters not be inquired into, or that the scope of the disclosure or discovery be limited to certain matters;

(5) that discovery be conducted with no one present except persons designated by the court;

(6) that a deposition, after being sealed, be opened only by order of the court;

(7) that a trade secret or other confidential research, development, or commercial information not be revealed or be revealed only in a designated way; and

(8) that the parties simultaneously file specified documents or information enclosed in sealed envelopes to be opened as directed by the court.

If the motion for a protective order is denied in whole or in part, the court may, on such terms and conditions as are just, order that any party or other person provide or permit discovery. The provisions of Rule 37(a)(4) apply to the award of expenses incurred in relation to the motion.

(d) Timing and Sequence of Discovery. Except in categories of proceedings exempted from initial disclosure under Rule 26(a)(1)(E), or when authorized under these rules or by order or agreement of the parties, a party may not seek discovery from any source before the parties have conferred as required by Rule 26(f). Unless the court upon motion, for the convenience of parties and witnesses and in the interests of justice, orders otherwise, methods of discovery may be used in any sequence, and the fact that a party is conducting discovery, whether by deposition or otherwise, does not operate to delay any other party's discovery.

(e) Supplementation of Disclosures and Responses. A party who has made a disclosure under subdivision (a) or responded to a request for discovery with a disclosure or response is under a duty to supplement or correct the disclosure or response to include information thereafter acquired if ordered by the court or in the following circumstances:

(1) A party is under a duty to supplement at appropriate intervals its disclosures under subdivision (a) if the party learns that in some material respect the information disclosed is incomplete or incorrect and if the additional or corrective information has not otherwise been made known to the other parties during the discovery process or in writing. With respect to testimony of an expert from whom a report is required un-

der subdivision (a)(2)(B) the duty extends both to information contained in the report and to information provided through a deposition of the expert, and any additions or other changes to this information shall be disclosed by the time the party's disclosures under Rule 26(a)(3) are due.

(2) A party is under a duty seasonably to amend a prior response to an interrogatory, request for production, or request for admission if the party learns that the response is in some material respect incomplete or incorrect and if the additional or corrective information has not otherwise been made known to the other parties during the discovery process or in writing.

(f) Conference of Parties; Planning for Discovery. Except in categories of proceedings exempted from initial disclosure under Rule 26(a)(1)(E) or when otherwise ordered, the parties must, as soon as practicable and in any event at least 21 days before a scheduling conference is held or a scheduling order is due under Rule 16(b), confer to consider the nature and basis of their claims and defenses and the possibilities for a prompt settlement or resolution of the case, to make or arrange for the disclosures required by Rule 26(a)(1), and to develop a proposed discovery plan that indicates the parties' views and proposals concerning:

(1) what changes should be made in the timing, form, or requirement for disclosures under Rule 26(a), including a statement as to when disclosures under Rule 26(a)(1) were made or will be made;

(2) the subjects on which discovery may be needed, when discovery should be completed, and whether discovery should be conducted in phases or be limited to or focused upon particular issues;

(3) what changes should be made in the limitations on discovery imposed under these rules or by local rule, and what other limitations should be imposed; and

(4) any other orders that should be entered by the court under Rule 26(c) or under Rule 16(b) and (c).

The attorneys of record and all unrepresented parties that have appeared in the case are jointly responsible for arranging the conference, for attempting in good faith to agree on the proposed discovery plan, and for submitting to the court within 14 days after the conference a written report outlining the plan. A court may order that the parties or attorneys attend the conference in person. If necessary to comply with its expedited schedule for Rule 16(b) conferences, a court may by local rule (i) require that the conference between the parties occur fewer than 21 days before the scheduling conference is held or a scheduling order is due under Rule 16(b), and (ii) require that the written report outlining the discovery plan be filed fewer than 14 days after the conference between the parties, or excuse the parties from submitting a written report and permit them to report orally on their discovery plan at the Rule 16(b) conference.

(g) Signing of Disclosures, Discovery Requests, Responses, and Objections.

(1) Every disclosure made pursuant to subdivision (a)(1) or subdivision (a)(3) shall be signed by at least one attorney of record in the attorney's individual name, whose address shall be stated. An unrepresented party shall sign the disclosure and state the party's address. The signature of the attorney or party constitutes a certification that to the best of the signer's knowledge, information, and belief, formed after a reasonable inquiry, the disclosure is complete and correct as of the time it is made.

(2) Every discovery request, response, or objection made by a party represented by an attorney shall be signed by at least one attorney of record in the attorney's individual name, whose address shall be stated. An unrepresented party shall sign the request, response, or objection and state the party's address. The signature of the attorney or party constitutes a certification that to the best of the signer's knowledge, information, and belief, formed after a reasonable inquiry, the request, response, or objection is:

(A) consistent with these rules and warranted by existing law or a good faith argument for the extension, modification, or reversal of existing law;

(B) not interposed for any improper purpose, such as to harass or to cause unnecessary delay or needless increase in the cost of litigation; and

(C) not unreasonable or unduly burdensome or expensive, given the needs of the case, the discovery already had in the case, the amount in controversy, and the importance of the issues at stake in the litigation.

If a request, response, or objection is not signed, it shall be stricken unless it is signed promptly after the omission is called to the attention of the party making the request, response, or objection, and a party shall not be obligated to take any action with respect to it until it is signed.

(3) If without substantial justification a certification is made in violation of the rule, the court, upon motion or upon its own initiative, shall impose upon the person who made the certification, the party on whose behalf the disclosure, request, response, or objection is made, or both, an appropriate sanction, which may include an order to pay the amount of the reasonable expenses incurred because of the violation, including a reasonable attorney's fee.

Commentary

By David A. Sonenshein
Temple University Beasley School of Law

Rule 26 sets forth the overarching provisions that define the scope and limitations of all of the discovery devices. Rule 26(b)(1) provides that the scope of discovery is broad, requiring only that the discovery sought be "relevant to the claim or defense of any party." (Prior to December 1, 2000, evidence could be discovered if it were merely "relevant to the subject matter of the pending action." After December 1, 2000, the court has discretion to extend the scope of relevance from "claim or defense" to the "subject matter" of the action.) To be discoverable, information need not be admissible at trial, as long as it is "reasonably calculated" to lead to the development of admissible evidence. Thus, for example, it is no objection at a deposition that a question simply calls for hearsay in the answer.

As a check on the breadth of discovery permitted by Rule 26(b)(1), Rule 26(b)(2) grants the court discretion to alter the limits on the number of depositions, requests to admit, and interrogatories as well as the length of depositions. Moreover, the court may otherwise regulate the frequency or extent of all discovery devices where the court finds: (1) the discovery is repetitive or unduly burdensome, (2) the party seeking discovery has wasted ample opportunity to obtain the information by other means, or (3) the burden of the proposed discovery outweighs its benefits.

In addition, Rule 26(b)(3) limits disclosure of work-product, i.e., documents or things prepared in anticipation of litigation by a party or its attorney (or representative as defined in the Rule). Such work product information is discoverable only upon the discoverer's meeting the rather stringent standard of "substantial need" for the information and the inability to obtain its equivalent without "undue hardship." Moreover, the Rule renders so-called "mental impression" work product, i.e., documents or things prepared for litigation which reveal the attorney's mental processes, strategy, conclusions, opinions, or theories, virtually undiscoverable absent a waiver of the work product immunity. Note that courts have ruled that waiver of even mental impression work product is possible where a witness refreshes his memory in preparation for trial or deposition with work product information. See Fed.R.Evid. 612 and *Sporck v. Peil*, 753 F.2d 312 (3rd Cir. 1985).

Finally, Rule 26(b)(4) provides virtual free access to the discovery by deposition of a "trial" or "testifying" expert, i.e., a person who will be qualified to testify at trial pursuant to Fed.R.Evid. 702, once the mandatory disclosure of the expert's opinion, basis, etc., has been made pursuant to Rule 26(a)(2). The Rule severely limits, however, discovery access to a "consulting expert," i.e., an expert who is retained to consult, but not testify. The consulting expert may not be discovered except upon an extraordinary showing of necessity and inability to obtain the same information elsewhere. A classic example of such a showing occurs where a consulting expert has performed a scientific analysis or test of a substance and the test has consumed all of the substance.

RULE 26. GENERAL PROVISIONS GOVERNING DISCOVERY; DUTY OF DISCLOSURE

Rule 26(b)(5) requires the party who resists discovery on grounds of privilege, work product or consulting expert trial preparation to make an express claim of the reason for withholding discovery and provide enough information regarding the basis or ground of the assertion (without disclosing its contents) to permit the other parties to the action to determine the applicability of the privilege or protection asserted.

Rule 26(c) provides the vehicle for the discoveree to seek a protective order for the purpose of shielding certain persons or information from discovery. The Rule requires the movant for the protective order to demonstrate that the discovery should be barred or limited to protect it from "annoyance, embarrassment, oppression, or undue burden or expense." The Rule lists a (non-exclusive) number of protective orders the court can issue, but courts will always balance the need for the discovery against the oppression it creates. Generally, real need for the discovery will trump the need for absolute protection.

According to Rule 26(d), parties may sequence and time their discovery as they see fit, assuming the parties first meet and confer as required by Rule 26(f) before commencing discovery.

Rule 26(e) requires parties who have made disclosures under Rule 26(a) or otherwise responded to discovery to supplement or correct their earlier-filed responses where the party discovers that the information earlier provided is incorrect or incomplete and the correct or previously omitted information has not been provided through subsequent discovery.

Rule 26(f) requires the parties to meet and confer at least fourteen days before a Rule 16(b) scheduling conference with the court or a scheduling order is due, for the purpose of discussing settlement, arranging for the mandatory disclosures required by Rule 26(a)(1), and developing a proposed discovery plan. The discovery plan should include the matters described in subdivisions (1)–(4) and must be forwarded to the court within ten days.

Rule 26(g) sets forth the signing and certification provisions for mandatory disclosures and discovery requests and responses. A signature of an attorney or unrepresented party on the disclosure constitutes a certification as to its completeness and correctness at the time. With respect to a discovery request, response, or objection, a signature constitutes a certification, formed after a reasonable inquiry, that the request, response, or objection is consistent with law or a good faith argument for the modification of existing law, not interposed for an improper purpose, and not unduly burdensome. If a certification is made in violation of this Rule without substantial justification, the court shall impose a sanction on the offending party that may include the opponent's expenses occasioned by the offending certification, including attorneys' fees.

Mandatory Disclosure (Rule 26(a))

In 1993, Rule 26(a) of the Federal Rules of Civil Procedure was radically amended to require "mandatory disclosure" by each party in the litigation of much of the information which historically (at least since the Federal Rules were promulgated in 1938) had been the subject of partisan discovery. Though one of the purposes of the amendment was to reduce parties' dependence on more costly traditional discovery by requiring the parties to provide each other with significant factual information without request from the opponent, it is hard to imagine that the parties will entirely forego additional discovery despite receiving the fruits of mandatory disclosure.

Overall, amended Rule 26(a) demands that all parties to the litigation provide all other parties with a variety of factual information which would ordinarily be discovered through discovery directed to fact and testifying expert witnesses. This information must be disclosed prior to, and irrespective of, any discovery request by an opponent or other party. Failure to comply with the mandatory disclosure requirements of Rule 26 subjects the non-producer to the panoply of sanctions contained in Rule 37(c) including preclusion of the non-producer from offering at trial evidence which should have been, but was not, disclosed at an early stage of the proceeding.

Rule 26(a) divides the mandatory disclosure process into three phases. The first phase is called "Initial Disclosures" and requires all parties to make the initial disclosure within ten days of the meeting of the parties to plan discovery mandated by Rule 26(f).

RULE 26. GENERAL PROVISIONS GOVERNING DISCOVERY; DUTY OF DISCLOSURE

With respect to timing, Rule 26(f) requires "... the parties shall, as soon as practicable and in any event at least 14 days before a scheduling conference is held or a scheduling order is due under Rule 16(b), meet to discuss the nature and basis of their claims and defenses ... to make or arrange for the disclosures required by subdivision (a)(1) [the initial disclosures], and to develop a proposed discovery plan." Because a Rule 16(b) scheduling conference must take place within ninety days of the defendant's filing of appearance or within 120 days of service of the complaint, the initial disclosures will ordinarily be due within a few months of the filing of the complaint.

Because the Initial Disclosures are required soon after the lawsuit is filed, it behooves the plaintiff to have prepared its Initial Disclosures before filing. This timing dovetails with the Rule 11 requirement that counsel make a reasonable inquiry into the facts that underlie a complaint prior to filing.

What is required to be disclosed at the initial stage of mandatory disclosure pursuant to Rule 26(a)(1) is clearly delineated. First, the parties must disclose the names, addresses, and telephone numbers of individuals "likely" to possess information relevant to those disputed facts that are alleged with particularity in the pleadings. Thus, under Rule 26(a)(1)(A), there is a premium on pleading allegations with specificity and particularity because those particularly plead allegations will draw initial disclosures from the other side.

Second, Rule 26(a)(1)(B) commands production of a copy or description of documents, tangible items, or other data compilations in the custody, control, or possession of the party which are relevant to disputed facts plead with particularity.

Third, Rule 26(a)(1)(C) requires disclosure of any damage computation which relates to any item of damage claimed by the disclosing party, including production of any unprivileged documents which contain such computation and/or relate to the "nature and extent of the damages suffered."

Fourth, Rule 26(a)(1)(D) commands production of any agreement of insurance that may be available to satisfy any judgment obtained in the lawsuit.

Finally, the parties cannot initiate the other forms of discovery until the Initial Disclosures are made.

In addition to the Initial Disclosures required by Rule 26(a)(1), Rule 26(a)(2) requires the parties to disclose, ninety days in advance of trial, the identity of their testifying experts and the expert's "detailed and complete" written report. According to the Rule the report shall contain a complete statement of all opinions to be expressed and the basis and reasons therefor; the data or other information considered by the witness in forming the opinions; any exhibits to be used as a summary of or support for the opinions; the qualifications of the witness, including a list of all publications authored by the witness within the preceding ten years; the compensation to be paid for the study and testimony; and a listing of any other cases in which the witness has testified as an expert at trial by deposition within the preceding four years.

Absent an agreement by the parties, a party may not take the deposition of a testifying expert until the mandatory disclosures pursuant to Rule 26(a)(2) are completed.

Finally, Rule 26(a)(3) requires additional "Pretrial Disclosures" shortly before trial. These additional disclosures include the identity and address of trial witnesses, designation of those witnesses whose testimony will be offered via deposition and pertinent portions of the deposition testimony, and identification of all exhibits that the parties intend to offer at trial.

Once the parties have met pursuant to Rule 16(f), the parties may proceed to the use of the other traditional discovery devices provided for in Rules 27–36. These devices include: (1) Interrogatories to parties found in FRCP 33, (2) Request for the production of documents to parties found in FRCP 34, (3) a Subpoena to nonparties for the production of documents or things found in FRCP 45, (4) Physical and mental examinations of persons who are parties or are in the control of a party found in FRCP 35, (5) Requests for admissions to parties found in FRCP 36, and (6) Depositions of parties and nonparties.

Rule 27. Depositions Before Action or Pending Appeal

(a) Before Action.

(1) Petition. A person who desires to perpetuate testimony regarding any matter that may be cognizable in any court of the United States may file a verified petition in the United States district court in the district of the residence of any expected adverse party. The petition shall be entitled in the name of the petitioner and shall show: 1, that the petitioner expects to be a party to an action cognizable in a court of the United States but is presently unable to bring it or cause it to be brought, 2, the subject matter of the expected action and the petitioner's interest therein, 3, the facts which the petitioner desires to establish by the proposed testimony and the reasons for desiring to perpetuate it, 4, the names or a description of the persons the petitioner expects will be adverse parties and their addresses so far as known, and 5, the names and addresses of the persons to be examined and the substance of the testimony which the petitioner expects to elicit from each, and shall ask for an order authorizing the petitioner to take the depositions of the persons to be examined named in the petition, for the purpose of perpetuating their testimony.

(2) Notice and Service. The petitioner shall thereafter serve a notice upon each person named in the petition as an expected adverse party, together with a copy of the petition, stating that the petitioner will apply to the court, at a time and place named therein, for the order described in the petition. At least 20 days before the date of hearing the notice shall be served either within or without the district or state in the manner provided in Rule 4(d) for service of summons; but if such service cannot with due diligence be made upon any expected adverse party named in the petition, the court may make such order as is just for service by publication or otherwise, and shall appoint, for persons not served in the manner provided in Rule 4(d), an attorney who shall represent them, and, in case they are not otherwise represented, shall cross-examine the deponent. If any expected adverse party is a minor or incompetent the provisions of Rule 17(c) apply.

(3) Order and Examination. If the court is satisfied that the perpetuation of the testimony may prevent a failure or delay of justice, it shall make an order designating or describing the persons whose depositions may be taken and specifying the subject matter of the examination and whether the depositions shall be taken upon oral examination or written interrogatories. The depositions may then be taken in accordance with these rules; and the court may make orders of the character provided for by Rules 34 and 35. For the purpose of applying these rules to depositions for perpetuating testimony, each reference therein to the court in which the action is pending shall be deemed to refer to the court in which the petition for such deposition was filed.

(4) Use of Deposition. If a deposition to perpetuate testimony is taken under these rules or if, although not so taken, it would be admissible in evidence in the courts of the state in which it is taken, it may be used in any action involving the same subject matter subsequently brought in a United States district court, in accordance with the provisions of Rule 32(a).

(b) Pending Appeal. If an appeal has been taken from a judgment of a district court or before the taking of an appeal if the time therefor has not expired, the district court in which the judgment was rendered may allow the taking of the depositions of witnesses to perpetuate their testimony for use in the event of further proceedings in the district court. In such case the party who desires to perpetuate the testimony may make a motion in the district court for leave to take the depositions, upon the same notice and service thereof as if the action was pending in the district court. The motion shall show (1) the names and addresses of persons to be examined and the substance of the testimony which the party expects to elicit from each; (2) the reasons for perpetuating their testimony. If the court finds that the perpetuation of the testimony is proper to avoid a failure or delay of justice, it may make an order allowing the depositions to be taken and may make orders of the character provided for by Rules 34 and 35, and thereupon the depositions may be taken and used in the same manner and under the same conditions as are prescribed in these rules for depositions taken in actions pending in the district court.

(c) Perpetuation by Action. This rule does not limit the power of a court to entertain an action to perpetuate testimony.

Commentary

By Linda G. Birchall
Powell, Goldstein, Frazer & Murphy

Rule 27 governs the taking of depositions and other "discovery" before a formal action has begun in the district courts and while an action is pending on appeal. Although Rule 27 also permits inspections of documents and things in addition to depositions—either upon oral examination or written questions—most courts have not allowed the Rule to serve as a vehicle for open discovery or as a fishing expedition for facts upon which a party can later form a cause of action. Rather, the primary purpose of Rule 27 "discovery," as opposed to normal discovery during the course of a lawsuit, is to allow parties, or potential parties, to preserve evidence that the parties are likely to need in a future proceeding before the district court. Such a deposition may be used like any other deposition taken during the ordinary course of discovery.

To request a deposition or inspection prior to an action pursuant to Rule 27(a), the party must file a verified petition in the district court and identify any other party that the movant expects to be a part of the future action. Although formal rules of jurisdiction and venue are not applicable because no formal lawsuit will have been filed, the movant must file the petition in the district court where any one of the expected parties resides. Rule 27(a)(1) sets forth five specific requirements for a petition: (1) expectation of a future action that cannot be filed at that time, (2) the subject matter of the expected action, (3) the general facts to be established and the reason for the deposition or inspection, (4) the identity of all expected parties to the future action, and (5) the identity of the proposed witness and the facts to be gained from his deposition. Section (a)(2) provides that the movant must attempt service of a notice of the deposition according to Rule 4(d) but allows the court to appoint an attorney to represent any party who could not be served.

Rule 28. Persons Before Whom Depositions May Be Taken

(a) **Within the United States.** Within the United States or within a territory or insular possession subject to the jurisdiction of the United States, depositions shall be taken before an officer authorized to administer oaths by the laws of the United States or of the place where the examination is held, or before a person appointed by the court in which the action is pending. A person so appointed has power to administer oaths and take testimony. The term officer as used in Rules 30, 31 and 32 includes a person appointed by the court or designated by the parties under Rule 29.

(b) **In Foreign Countries.** Depositions may be taken in a foreign country (1) pursuant to any applicable treaty or convention, or (2) pursuant to a letter of request (whether or not captioned a letter rogatory), or (3) on notice before a person authorized to administer oaths in the place where the examination is held, either by the law thereof or by the law of the United States, or (4) before a person commissioned by the court, and a person so commissioned shall have the power by virtue of the commission to administer any necessary oath and take testimony. A commission or a letter of request shall be issued on application and notice and on terms that are just and appropriate. It is not requisite to the issuance of a commission or a letter of request that the taking of the deposition in any other manner is impracticable or inconvenient; and both a commission and a letter of request may be issued in proper cases. A notice or commission may designate the person before whom the deposition is to be taken either by name or descriptive title. A letter of request may be addressed "To the Appropriate Authority in [here name the country]." When a letter of request or any other device is used pursuant to any applicable treaty or convention, it shall be captioned in the form prescribed by that treaty or convention. Evidence obtained in response to a letter of request need not be excluded merely because it is not a verbatim transcript, because the testimony was not taken under oath, or because of any similar departure from the requirements for depositions taken within the United States under these rules.

(c) **Disqualification for Interest.** No deposition shall be taken before a person who is a relative or employee or attorney or counsel of any of the parties, or is a relative or employee of such attorney or counsel, or is financially interested in the action.

Commentary

By Linda G. Birchall
Powell, Goldstein, Frazer & Murphy

Depositions taken in the United States are treated differently than those taken in foreign countries. Rule 28 describes the individuals before whom a deposition may be taken and, for foreign depositions, the procedures for taking the deposition. For depositions taken in the United States, Rule 28(a) allows an officer authorized to administer oaths or anyone appointed by the court, assuming the individual has no interest in the underlying action, to record or transcribe the deposition.

Outside the United States, however, the procedures are more complicated. Rule 28(b) sets forth the four particular methods now used to authorize a deposition in a foreign country. The four options are: (1) pursuant to a treaty or convention; (2) pursuant to a letter of request; (3) upon notice and before someone authorized, by either U.S. law or the law of the jurisdiction, to administer oaths in that jurisdiction; and (4) before someone commissioned by the district court. Under the final option, the commission by the district court empowers the individual to administer any necessary oaths.

These options were designed to offer increased flexibility not available in the original rule. Despite the enhanced flexibility, however, Rule 28(b) does not automatically authorize a deposition in any foreign jurisdiction, even if a party attempts to comply with one of the four accepted procedures. There still exist many foreign jurisdictions in which depositions are not permissible for use in a court outside of that jurisdiction, such as a United States district court. Rule 28(b), therefore, merely provides the correct procedures where depositions are already permitted.

The amendments to Rule 28(b) that added flexibility also removed some discretion from the district courts. Now, a United States court "shall" issue a letter of request or a commission for a foreign deposition upon a proper application. Those procedures are no longer reserved for situations where the deposition would otherwise be virtually impossible or impractical. Nevertheless, Rule 28(b) should be limited to the testimony of fact witnesses and should not be utilized to obtain deposition testimony from foreign expert witnesses unless absolutely necessary.

Although letters of request are ordinarily routed through the United States Department of State to the appropriate foreign authority, the judge may issue a letter of request directly to the foreign authority. If issued pursuant to a particular treaty or convention, the letter must be captioned in the form prescribed by the applicable treaty or convention and should be addressed as, "To the Appropriate Authority in [name of country]," unless the issuing judge already knows the particular authority for that country.

Importantly, because of the different procedures used for recording a deposition in many foreign jurisdictions, Rule 28(b) provides for expanded use of depositions taken pursuant to letters of request. Whereas most depositions must comply with requirements under the Federal Rules of Civil Procedure, Rule 28(b) expressly states that a deposition taken pursuant to a letter of request may still be used even if it is not under oath, is not a verbatim transcript, or if it is otherwise defective.

Whether in the United States or in a foreign jurisdiction, Rule 28(c) specifically prohibits any individual from administering the deposition if that individual is related to any party or counsel, or if the individual has any financial interest in the underlying action.

Rule 29. Stipulations Regarding Discovery Procedure

Unless otherwise directed by the court, the parties may by written stipulation (1) provide that depositions may be taken before any person, at any time or place, upon any notice, and in any manner and when so taken may be used like other depositions, and (2) modify other procedures governing or limitations placed upon discovery, except that stipulations extending the time provided in Rules 33, 34, and 36 for responses to discovery may, if they would interfere with any time set for completion of discovery, for hearing of a motion, or for trial, be made only with the approval of the court.

Commentary

By Linda G. Birchall
Powell, Goldstein, Frazer & Murphy

Notwithstanding the formal procedures and requirements set forth by these Federal Rules of Civil Procedure to govern discovery, Rule 29 grants the parties to an action permission to modify most of the rules and procedures by stipulation. As stated by the Advisory Committee in the 1993 amendment to Rule 29, the parties may now "agree on less expensive and time-consuming methods to obtain information" relevant to the lawsuit. For instance, under Rule 29(1), the parties may stipulate that depositions may be taken before any person, at any place, and in any manner, yet still be used as if all formal requirements have been satisfied. Such stipulations may further ease the burdens of taking depositions in foreign jurisdictions even beyond the flexibility of Rule 28(b), assuming, however, that the foreign jurisdiction permits the depositions to be taken at all.

Subsection (2) of Rule 29 extends the power to modify procedures by stipulation to all forms of discovery. By virtue of the final clause of Rule 29, however, the court retains the power to overrule or disallow any stipulation that would interfere with the discovery period or the time set for hearings or trial. According to the language of the Rule and the Advisory Committee notes, the parties should obtain prior approval for any such stipulations that would interfere with the court's schedules.

Rule 30. Depositions Upon Oral Examination

(a) When Depositions May Be Taken; When Leave Required.

(1) A party may take the testimony of any person, including a party, by deposition upon oral examination without leave of court except as provided in paragraph (2). The attendance of witnesses may be compelled by subpoena as provided in Rule 45.

(2) A party must obtain leave of court, which shall be granted to the extent consistent with the principles stated in rule 26(b)(2), if the person to be examined is confined in prison or if, without the written stipulation of the parties,

> (A) a proposed deposition would result in more than ten depositions being taken under this rule or Rule 31 by the plaintiffs, or by the defendants, or by third-party defendants;

> (B) the person to be examined already has been deposed in the case; or

> (C) a party seeks to take a deposition before the time specified in Rule 26(d) unless the notice contains a certification, with supporting facts, that the person to be examined is expected to leave the United States and be unavailable for examination in this country unless deposed before that time.

(b) Notice of Examination: General Requirements; Method of Recording; Production of Documents and Things; Deposition of Organization; Deposition by Telephone.

(1) A party desiring to take the deposition of any person upon oral examination shall give reasonable notice in writing to every other party to the action. The notice shall state the time and place for taking the deposition and the name and address of each person to be examined, if known, and, if the name is not known, a general description sufficient to identify the person or the particular class or group to which the person belongs. If a subpoena duces tecum is to be served on the person to be examined, the designation of the materials to be produced as set

forth in the subpoena shall be attached to, or included in, the notice.

(2) The party taking the deposition shall state in the notice the method by which the testimony shall be recorded. Unless the court orders otherwise, it may be recorded by sound, sound-and-visual, or stenographic means, and the party taking the deposition shall bear the cost of the recording. Any party may arrange for a transcription to be made from the recording of a deposition taken by nonstenographic means.

(3) With prior notice to the deponent and other parties, any party may designate another method to record the deponent's testimony in addition to the method specified by the person taking the deposition. The additional record or transcript shall be made at that party's expense unless the court otherwise orders.

(4) Unless otherwise agreed by the parties, a deposition shall be conducted before an officer appointed or designated under Rule 28 and shall begin with a statement on the record by the officer that includes (A) the officer's name and business address; (B) the date, time and place of the deposition; (C) the name of the deponent; (D) the administration of the oath or affirmation to the deponent; and (E) an identification of all persons present. If the deposition is recorded other than steno- graphically, the officer shall repeat items (A) through (C) at the beginning of each unit of recorded tape or other recording medium. The appearance or demeanor of deponents or attor- neys shall not be distorted through camera or sound- recording techniques. At the end of the deposition, the officer shall state on the record that the deposition is complete and shall set forth any stipulations made by counsel concerning the custody of the transcript or recording and the exhibits, or concerning other pertinent matters.

(5) The notice to a party deponent may be accompanied by a request made in compliance with for the production of docu- ments and tangible things at the taking of the deposition. The procedure of shall apply to the request.

(6) A party may in the party's notice and in a subpoena name as the deponent a public or private corporation or a partnership or association or governmental agency and describe with reasonable particularity the matters on which examination is requested. In that event, the organization so named shall designate one or more officers, directors, or managing agents, or other persons who consent to testify on its behalf, and may set forth, for each person designated, the matters on which the person will testify. A subpoena shall advise a non-party organization of its duty to make such a designation. The persons so designated shall testify as to matters known or reasonably available to the organization. This subdivision (b)(6) does not preclude taking a deposition by any other procedure authorized in these rules.

(7) The parties may stipulate in writing or the court may upon motion order that a deposition be taken by telephone or other remote electronic means. For the purposes of this rule and Rules 28(a), 37(a)(1), and 37(b)(1), a deposition taken by such means is taken in the district and at the place where the deponent is to answer questions.

(c) **Examination and Cross-Examination; Record of Examination; Oath; Objections.** Examination and cross-examination of witnesses may proceed as permitted at the trial under the provisions of the Federal Rules of Evidence except Rules 103 and 615. The officer before whom the deposition is to be taken shall put the witness on oath or affirmation and shall personally, or by someone acting under the officer's direction and in the officer's presence, record the testimony of the witness. The testimony shall be taken stenographically or recorded by any other method authorized by subdivision (b)(2) of this rule. All objections made at the time of the examination to the qualifications of the officer taking the deposition, to the manner of taking it, to the evidence presented, to the conduct of any party, or to any other aspect of the proceedings shall be noted by the officer upon the record of the deposition; but the examination shall proceed, with the testimony being taken subject to the objections. In lieu of participating in the oral examination, parties may serve written questions in a sealed envelope on the party taking the deposition and the party taking the deposition shall transmit them to the officer, who shall propound them to the witness and record the answers verbatim.

(d) Schedule and Duration; Motion to Terminate or Limit Examination.

(1) Any objection during a deposition must be stated concisely and in a non-argumentative and non-suggestive manner. A person may instruct a deponent not to answer only when necessary to preserve a privilege, to enforce a limitation directed by the court, or to present a motion under Rule 30(d)(4).

(2) Unless otherwise authorized by the court or stipulated by the parties, a deposition is limited to one day of seven hours. The court must allow additional time consistent with Rule 26(b)(2) if needed for a fair examination of the deponent or if the deponent or another person, or other circumstance, impedes or delays the examination.

(3) If the court finds that any impediment, delay, or other conduct has frustrated the fair examination of the deponent, it may impose upon the persons responsible an appropriate sanction, including the reasonable costs and attorney's fees incurred by any parties as a result thereof.

(4) At any time during a deposition, on motion of a party or of the deponent and upon a showing that the examination is being conducted in bad faith or in such manner as unreasonably to annoy, embarrass, or oppress the deponent or party, the court in which the action is pending or the court in the district where the deposition is being taken may order the officer conducting the examination to cease forthwith from taking the deposition, or may limit the scope and manner of the taking of the deposition as provided in Rule 26(c). If the order made terminates the examination, it may be resumed thereafter only upon the order of the court in which the action is pending. Upon demand of the objecting party or deponent, the taking of the deposition must be suspended for the time necessary to make a motion for an order. The provisions of Rule 37(a)(4) apply to the award of expenses incurred in relation to the motion.

(e) Review by Witness; Changes; Signing. If requested by the deponent or a party before completion of the deposition, the deponent shall have 30 days after being notified by the officer that the transcript or recording is available in which to review the transcript or recording and, if there are changes in form or substance, to sign a statement reciting such changes and the reasons given by the deponent for making them. The officer shall indicate in the certificate prescribed by subdivision (f)(1) whether any review was requested and, if so, shall append any changes made by the deponent during the period allowed.

(f) Certification and Delivery by Officer; Exhibits; Copies.

(1) The officer must certify that the witness was duly sworn by the officer and that the deposition is a true record of the testimony given by the witness. This certificate must be in writing and accompany the record of the deposition. Unless otherwise ordered by the court, the officer must securely seal the deposition in an envelope or package indorsed with the title of the action and marked "Deposition of [here insert name of witness]" and must promptly send it to the attorney who arranged for the transcript or recording, who must store it under conditions that will protect it against loss, destruction, tampering, or deterioration. Documents and things produced for inspection during the examination of the witness must, upon the request of a party, be marked for identification and annexed to the deposition and may be inspected and copied by any party, except that if the person producing the materials desires to retain them the person may (A) offer copies to be marked for identification and annexed to the deposition and to serve thereafter as originals if the person affords to all parties fair opportunity to verify the copies by comparison with the originals, or (B) offer the originals to be marked for identification, after giving to each party an opportunity to inspect and copy them, in which event the materials may then be used in the same manner as if annexed to the deposition. Any party may move for an order that the original be annexed to and returned with the deposition to the court, pending final disposition of the case.

(2) Unless otherwise ordered by the court or agreed by the parties, the officer shall retain stenographic notes of any deposition taken stenographically or a copy of the recording of any deposition taken by another method. Upon payment of reasonable charges therefor, the officer shall furnish a copy of the transcript or other recording of the deposition to any party or

to the deponent.

(3) The party taking the deposition shall give prompt notice of its filing to all other parties.

(g) Failure to Attend or to Serve Subpoena; Expenses.

(1) If the party giving the notice of the taking of a deposition fails to attend and proceed therewith and another party attends in person or by attorney pursuant to the notice, the court may order the party giving the notice to pay to such other party the reasonable expenses incurred by that party and that party's attorney in attending, including reasonable attorney's fees.

(2) If the party giving the notice of the taking of a deposition of a witness fails to serve a subpoena upon the witness and the witness because of such failure does not attend, and if another party attends in person or by attorney because that party expects the deposition of that witness to be taken, the court may order the party giving the notice to pay to such other party the reasonable expenses incurred by that party and that party's attorney in attending, including reasonable attorney's fees.

Commentary

By David A. Sonenshein
Temple University Beasley School of Law

FRCP 30 governs the notice and taking of depositions. FRCP 30 was extensively revised in 1993, along with FRCP 26 and 32, in order to modernize deposition practice to accommodate advances in technology, to promote the reduction of litigation costs, and to foster a more professional practice. The Rule should be read in conjunction with FRCP 26, which provides the framework for the scope of all discovery in civil matters in United States district courts. Practitioners should also consult the local rules of court because the various districts may alter certain provisions of both FRCP 26 and 32.

Part (a) of the Rule governs when depositions may be taken and the exceptional circumstances when leave of court is required. Essentially, any party may take the deposition of a witness at any time after the parties have met and conferred as required under

FRCP 26(f) and exchanged the "initial disclosures" mandated in FRCP 26(a). The deposing party should subpoena all nonparty witnesses pursuant to FRCP; otherwise, a witness who fails to appear will not be subject to sanctions. However, the deposing party need not subpoena a duly noticed party-witness to attend a deposition. Failure of the party-witness to attend a duly noticed deposition will trigger sanctions.

FRCP 30(a) also limits each party in the lawsuit to ten depositions of one day's duration (7 hours) each, but provides that relief from these limitations may be granted by agreement of the parties or by leave of court. In addition, leave of court is required to re-depose any witness or depose a witness prior to the time specified in FRCP 26(d).

Part (b) of the Rule deals with notice procedures. FRCP 30(b)(1) provides that the party desiring to take a deposition must give "reasonable notice in writing to every other party to the action" in the totality of the circumstances. At least one court has ruled that two-day advance notice is unreasonable per se. Further, the practitioner should consult local rules and the code of conduct or professionalism within the jurisdiction, which may set out specific notice requirements, including prior consultation with opposing counsel.

If the deposition taker desires a nonparty deponent to bring documents or things with him to the deposition, a subpoena duces tecum must be attached to the deposition subpoena. If the deponent is a party, the deposition taker may append a FRCP 34 Request for the Production of Documents or Things to the Notice of Deposition.

FRCP 30(b)(2) and (3) provide that the party taking the deposition shall state in the notice the means, stenographic or non-stenographic (including videotape), by which the deposition will be transcribed (at the cost to the deposition taker). Any other party, on notice to the deponent and the other parties, may designate any other additional method of transcription at the noticing party's expense. Thus, for example, any party may videotape any deposition without leave of court or agreement from its opponents or co-parties.

FRCP 30(b)(6) Depositions

Often, a party seeking discovery from a corporation, government agency, or other organization does not know the identity of the person or persons within the organization who have knowledge of discoverable facts. In such event, FRCP 30(b)(6) provides that one seeking discovery may name as a deponent, in either the party notice or in a nonparty subpoena, the corporation, agency, or other organization and describe with particularity the matters on which examination is demanded. Upon receipt of such a notice or subpoena, the discoveree organization is obligated to select and produce for deposition, officers, directors, managing agents, or any other person with knowledge of the particularized information. The deponent produced must consent to be deposed and the organization must designate the matters upon which each person produced will testify. In the event the discoveree organization is a nonparty, the FRCP 30(b)(6) subpoena must inform the nonparty of its obligation to designate deponents.

The designated deponent must testify to matters known and "reasonably available to the organization" as well. Though the designating organization need not produce the person who is the most knowledgeable in the organization about the subjects of the deposition, the organization has the good faith obligation to name a person or persons who possess sufficient knowledge to respond accurately to any questions within the scope of the matters included within the notice of deposition. If the person designated cannot provide answers to matters specified in the notice or subpoena, the organization is obliged to substitute another person immediately who can provide such information.

The designated persons may, but need not, be officers, directors, or managing agents or even employees of the organization, but the deposed organization must prepare the designated deponent so that he is able to "give complete, knowledgeable, and binding answers on behalf of the corporation."

Courts will sanction the organization's failure to designate an adequate representative or substitute for an inadequate representative because when a corporation or association designates a person to testify on its behalf, the corporation appears vicariously through that person. If the person is not knowledgeable about the relevant facts, and the principal has failed to designate an available, knowledgeable, and readily identifiable witness, then the appearance is, for all practical purposes, no appearance at all.

The 30(b)(6) procedure is distinguishable from the situation where the deposing party seeks to depose a particular person associated with an organization. The deposing party may subpoena such a person like any other witness, but such a person is not designated to testify on behalf of the corporation in the way that a 30(b)(6) deponent would. Thus, the deposing party cannot notice the organization pursuant to FRCP 30(b)(6) and then insist that the organization designate a particular person to testify on its behalf pursuant to 30(b)(6). The organization will be required to produce an officer, director, or managing agent, however, pursuant to FRCP 30(b)(6).

The Procedure for Organizational Depositions

Where the organization is a party, the 30(b)(6) notice of deposition is sufficient to force the organization to comply and designate a deponent with knowledge. The notice is similar to the ordinary FRCP 30(b)(1) notice except that it includes a general description of the person to be designated and a reasonably particular description of the matters on which to inquire. In addition, the notice advises the organization of its obligation to designate the person or persons who consent to be deposed on behalf of the organization. A subpoena is unnecessary when seeking the 30(b)(6) deposition of a party-organization. Pursuant to FRCP 32(a)(2), the deposing party may use the deposition of the adverse party's 30(b)(6) designee for any purpose at trial, including the truth.

Pursuant to FRCP 30(b)(1), the only people considered to be parties when the party is an organization are officers, directors, and managing agents of the organization. These persons can be noticed individually and by name to be deposed, and failure of the organization-party to produce officers, directors, or managing agents after proper notice to all parties is sanctionable pursuant to FRCP 37(d)(1). Finally, pursuant to FRCP 32(a)(2), the deposing party may use the deposition of "anyone who at the time of taking the deposition was an officer, director, or managing agent" of the adverse party-organization for any purpose including the truth at trial.

While the identity of officers and directors is usually easy to ascertain, the identification of a managing agent can be more problematic. Though courts make this determination on a case-by-case basis, they apply a general test, examining whether the purported managing agent: (1) is given the power by the organization to exercise his discretion in dealing with corporate matters, (2) can be depended upon to follow the employer's wishes and give testimony pursuant to his employer's opponent's demand, and (3) can be expected to identify the organization's interests rather than those of the opposing party. The third and last consideration has been deemed the "paramount test" by a number of courts.

The practical effects of the determination that an employee of a corporation is a "managing agent" are: (1) that the corporation must produce the employee for examination at its own expense, (2) that the employee's deposition may be used for any purpose at trial, and (3) that the corporation's pleadings may be stricken if the employee willfully fails to appear before the officer who is to take the deposition.

If the employee is not a managing agent, officer, or director, the employee is treated as an ordinary nonparty witness who must be subpoenaed to guarantee attendance at the deposition, and whose failure to appear can lead to a sanction of the person, but not the party by which that person is employed. A person who is not a managing agent, officer, or director, who is designated pursuant to FRCP 30(b)(6), however, does speak for the organization if he consents to testify at the deposition.

Pursuant to FRCP 30(b)(6), where the party-organization designates an ordinary employee, i.e., a person who is not an officer, director, or managing agent, to testify on the organization's behalf, the employee who has an independent or conflicting interest in the litigation—for example, in a personal injury case—can refuse to testify on behalf of the organization.

If the designated person does not consent to be a 30(b)(6) deponent, that person is treated as a nonparty and his attendance must be procured by subpoena in accordance with FRCP 45. Absent unavailability pursuant to FRCP 32(a), his deposition is not admissible at trial for the truth against the party-organization, the party-organization is not sanctioned for a failure to appear or cooperate at the deposition, and the deposing party must pay the expense of procuring attendance.

Limiting the Scope of the 30(b)(6) Deposition

The scope of a 30(b)(6) deposition includes at least those matters set forth with reasonable particularity in the notice of deposition or subpoena. If deposing counsel confine themselves to questioning of those matters and avoid seeking privileged information, then the deponent must answer all questions. If, however, deposing counsel move beyond the matters described in the notice or subpoena, defending counsel must be careful because the 30(b)(6) deponent's answers will be admissible against the organization.

If counsel would like to foreclose questioning beyond the scope of the notice or subpoena, he may object on that ground and will be sustained by most courts. *Paparelli v. Prudential Insurance Co.*, 108 F.R.D. 727 (D. Mass 1985) is instructive. In *Paparelli*, defending counsel objected to questions relating to a document that counsel claimed exceeded the scope of the notice. In response, deposing counsel argued that though his questions did exceed the scope of his notice, a 30(b)(6) deponent must answer any question about which he has knowledge that relates to the subject matter of the lawsuit.

In sustaining the deponent in not answering questions which exceed the scope of the notice, the *Paparelli* court explained that "[i]f a party were free to ask any questions, even if 'relevant' to the lawsuit, which were completely outside the scope of 'matters on which examination is requested,' the requirement that the matters be listed 'with reasonable particularity' would make no sense." The court also reasoned from the Advisory Committee Notes that because an organization is required, pursuant to FRCP 30(b)(6) to prepare a person to testify as to matters duly designated in the notice, it would be unfair and unduly burdensome to require preparation for all matters, whether or not referenced in the notice. Likewise, it would not be fair to bind the corporation by the testimony of an employee (other than a director, officer, or managing agent) speaking about matters beyond the scope of either the notice or the designated employee's authority.

There is contrary authority that holds that the 30(b)(6) designee can be required to answer questions beyond the scope of the notice. In *King v. Pratt & Whitney*, 161 F.R.D. 475 (S.D. Fla. 1995), the plaintiff served the defendant corporation three notices pursuant to FRCP 30(b)(6), requesting the corporation to designate representatives to testify on three separate matters in the litigation. When the representatives were queried on matters beyond the scope of the respective notices, defending counsel instructed the deponents not to answer the questions, adjourned the depositions, and sought protective orders limiting the scope of the issues at the depositions to the matters specifically described in the notices.

Framing the issue as "whether a deponent produced pursuant to a FRCP 30(b)(6) notice may only be questioned regarding those issues described in the notice or may be questioned as broadly as any other deponent," the court ruled that the designee can be questioned like any other deponent. The court explained that the Rule's requirement of particularity in describing the issues for the deposition is designed to aid the corporate party in selecting the appropriate representative, but imposes no limit on the questioning of the designee beyond what is available for any deponent as governed by Rule 30(b)(1). After all, the court reasoned, FRCP 30(b)(6) does not preclude the taking of a separate deposition of the witness designated by the corporation by the usual deposition rules. Therefore, the court concluded that if the examining party asks questions outside the scope of the notice, the usual deposition rules apply and the scope objection is unavailing.

Given the uncertainty of a court's ruling on the issue of the scope of the 30(b)(6) deposition, it would seem to be wise for the deposing party to serve a notice or subpoena on the person designated pursuant to FRCP 30(b)(6) (if identified before the 30(b)(6) deposition) so that the deposition examination can venture beyond the scope of the notice. It would behoove the deposition defender to demand that any questions asked beyond the scope (assuming the defender's instruction not to answer and motion for protective order is overruled by the court) be segregated at the end of the record so that a jury or court can consider the "beyond the scope" questions as answered in the witness's individual capacity, separately from the testimony which binds the organization pursuant to FRCP 30(b)(6).

Sequestration of Deponents

The 1993 revisions to Part (c) of the Rule clarify the law regarding the sequestration of deponents. Specifically, the deposition examination is to proceed as permitted at trial in accordance with the Federal Rules of Evidence, except that FRE 103 and 615 do not apply to deposition testimony. Accordingly, absent a showing of "good cause" a future deponent cannot be excluded from another's deposition. Though there is no right of the press or strangers to attend a deposition, parties, witnesses, or others can only be excluded on a showing of "good cause."

Objections and Instructions Not to Answer

FRCP 30(c) and (d) set forth the procedure for objections and instructions not to answer questions at depositions. Any objection to evidence or any other aspect of the taking of the deposition must be made on the record and will be noted by the reporter, but answers will be required to any question except in three particular situations. First, counsel may instruct his witness not to answer a question at a deposition that will reveal privileged information. Second, counsel may instruct a witness not to answer a deposition question where a court has already directed by protective order that such answers not be given. Third, counsel may instruct a witness not to answer a question which seeks information which could be the subject of a protective order or is asked in bad faith and/or in such a manner which is unreasonable in annoying, oppressing, or harassing the deponent or party. In the event that counsel does instruct his client not to answer a deposition question, counsel is obligated to forthwith seek a protective order or risk waiver of the objection.

Counsel is generally not permitted to speak with his deponent-client while a question is pending except for the purpose of discussion of one of the three above-mentioned instructions not to answer.

Though counsel who is defending the deposition need not object to issues of relevance, hearsay, or other matters of substantive admissibility of evidence, counsel is required, on risk of waiver at trial, to object at the deposition to the impermissible form of the question or to any other question where an objection could cure the problem in the question and make the answer admissible (for example, an improper or insufficient foundation). Thus, defending counsel will be obligated, absent a contrary stipulation, to make at least the following objections: leading (except as to an opposing party), misleading (assumes facts not in evidence), compound or multifarious, narrative, vague, argumentative, misquoting the witness, asked and answered, improper opinion or conclusion, or lack of foundation. The Rules forbid "speaking objections," i.e., objections that go beyond stating the ground of the objection and suggest the preferred answer to the deponent. Note, some local district court rules confine objecting counsel to objecting on the ground of "the form of the question," thus forbidding even the stating of the ground of the objection for the record.

FRCP 30(e) Procedures

FRCP 30(e) provides for the review, correction, reading, and signing of the deposition transcript by the deponent. The Rule requires reading and signing of the transcript within 30 days of notification of its transcription only if the deponent or any party requests it before completion of the deposition. Unlike the practice before the 1993 amendments to FRCP 30, a transcript is not "deemed" read and signed unless it really is. The vast majority of courts permit the deponent to make any changes to his deposition answers. A few courts, however, limit the changes to so-called "scrivener's errors," i.e., typographical errors. In any event, all corrections or changes must be accompanied by a signed statement of the reasons for the change(s).

FRCP 30(f) Procedures

Pursuant to FRCP 30(f), the officer taking the deposition need not file it with the court but rather may send it to the attorney who arranged for the transcript or recording. Under these circumstances, the practitioner is obligated to store it under conditions that will protect it against loss, destruction, tampering or deterioration. The lawyer retaining the deposition must also retain and preserve the exhibits. However, the party or witness who originally produced the exhibits may retain the originals unless the court orders that the original exhibit be annexed to the deposition and returned to the court pending final disposition of the case.

Rule 31. Depositions Upon Written Questions

(a) Serving Questions; Notice.

(1) A party may take the testimony of any person, including a party, by deposition upon written questions without leave of court except as provided in paragraph (2). The attendance of witnesses may be compelled by the use of subpoena as provided in Rule 45.

(2) A party must obtain leave of court, which shall be granted to the extent consistent with the principles stated in Rule 26(b)(2), if the person to be examined is confined in prison or if, without the written stipulation of the parties.

(A) a proposed deposition would result in more than ten depositions being taken under this rule or Rule 30 by the plaintiffs, or by the defendants, or by third-party defendants;

(B) the person to be examined has already been deposed in the case; or

(C) a party seeks to take a deposition before the time specified in Rule 26(d).

(3) A party desiring to take a deposition upon written questions shall serve them upon every other party with a notice stating (1) the name and address of the person who is to answer them, if known, and if the name is not known, a general description sufficient to identify the person or the particular class or group to which the person belongs, and (2) the name or descriptive title and address of the officer before whom the deposition is to be taken. A deposition upon written questions may be taken of a public or private corporation or a partnership or association or governmental agency in accordance with the provisions of Rule 30(b)(6).

(4) Within 14 days after the notice and written questions are served, a party may serve cross-questions upon all other parties. Within 7 days after being served with cross-questions, a party may serve redirect questions upon all other parties. Within

7 days after being served with redirect questions, a party may serve recross-questions upon all other parties. The court may for cause shown enlarge or shorten the time.

(b) Officer to Take Responses and Prepare Record. A copy of the notice and copies of all questions served shall be delivered by the party taking the deposition to the officer designated in the notice, who shall proceed promptly, in the manner provided by Rule 30(c), (e), and (f), to take the testimony of the witness in response to the questions and to prepare, certify, and file or mail the deposition, attaching thereto the copy of the notice and the questions received by the officer.

(c) Notice of Filing. When the deposition is filed the party taking it shall promptly give notice thereof to all other parties.

Commentary

By Shane Read
U.S. Attorney's Office, Northern District of Texas

Rule 31 provides that a party may take the testimony of a party or any other person through the use of written questions as opposed to an oral deposition. Depositions by written questions are infrequently used, but they can be advantageous in certain circumstances. As with oral depositions (Rule 30), the attendance of witnesses may be compelled by subpoena as provided by Rule 45.

In general, leave of court is not required in order to take a deposition upon written questions. Leave of court is required if: (1) the person to be examined is in prison; (2) the proposed deposition will exceed the ten depositions which are allowed by each side; (3) the person to be deposed has already given a deposition; or (4) the party seeks to take a deposition before the discovery planning meeting as set forth in Rule 26(f).

A notice must accompany the written questions and that notice must include the name and address of the deponent (or a definitive description if the name is not known, e.g., custodian of medical records), and the name and descriptive title and address of the court reporter before whom the deposition will be taken. The notice must be served on all parties. FRCP 28 sets out the officers before whom a deposition can be taken in the United States and the process in foreign countries.

After the notice and written questions have been served, a party has fourteen days to serve cross-questions upon all other parties. Then, the party wanting to take the deposition has a seven-day interval in order to respond with redirect questions followed by another seven-day interval in which the responding party may serve recross-questions. A cautionary point: although a party has seven days to respond with another round of questions (i.e., recross-questions), a party has only five days to serve objections to the form of previously served questions or those objections are waived (see Rule 32(d)(3)(C)).

After the questions and any objections have been served, the party wanting to take the deposition must deliver a copy of the notice and copies of all questions to the court reporter identified in the notice. The court reporter must then promptly take the testimony of the witness (in compliance with Rule 30(c) oath and recording, (e) review by witness, and (f) certification and filing). This process involves the court reporter reading the questions to the witness and taking down the answers in transcript form as if it were an oral deposition. As with an oral deposition, the court reporter then submits the transcript to the witnesses for their review and signature. The court reporter files, mails, or certifies the transcript. When the deposition is filed, the party taking it shall promptly give notice to all other parties. The court reporter then prepares, certifies, and files or mails the deposition.

In general there are more disadvantages than advantages to taking a deposition upon written questions. The most obvious problem is that there is no way to follow up on answers given by the deponent that may lead to other important information. Moreover, if the witness's answer is ambiguous, there will be no way to clarify the response. Equally troubling is that if the witness gives an evasive answer or complains that he does not understand the question, there is no chance to rephrase the question or compel an answer. Finally, given that the other side will know the questions in advance, any hope of surprise will be lost.

Having said that, Rule 31 can be a powerful and useful tool. It is underutilized and very useful for getting medical and business records admitted at trial. For example, a party could send out a Notice of Deposition Upon Written Questions with a subpoena duces tecum to the custodian of medical records. The written questions could establish the deponent as a record custodian and then questions could be asked regarding the documents brought by the custodian to the deposition (which are responsive to the subpoena duces tecum) so that the documents could meet the hearsay exception for business records. Having conducted such a deposition, the party would then be able to call the custodian at trial and have the records admitted.

It is effective to use Rule 31 when one is comfortable that the deponent will give favorable testimony. The process prevents opposing counsel from effectively cross-examining your witness.

An attractive characteristic of the use of a deposition by written questions is its cost effectiveness. For example, if a party in a personal injury case needs to secure the testimony of a treating physician, FRCP 31 can save money. Oftentimes treating doctors will charge an hourly rate for an oral deposition (currently around $1,000/hr) and the use of written questions will greatly reduce costs.

Another underutilized area where deposition by written questions should be used is where witnesses are a great distance from the jurisdiction in which the lawsuit is filed. Written questions provide the opportunity for the party taking the deposition to avoid the costs of time and travel in taking an oral deposition.

Remember that it is important to speak to the witness prior to sending written questions in order to ensure that one is preserving favorable testimony instead of memorializing something one will regret at trial.

Similarly, the increased internationalization of trade means more witnesses will be in a foreign country, and FRCP 31 may be the best and most cost effective tool to gather and preserve the facts. An added note of caution, however, is that an attorney must understand exactly what is likely to happen in a foreign country during the response to the written questions. Local customs and relationships may insert unanticipated bias, and retaining local counsel may be necessary to understand and produce the results needed.

And finally on an administrative note, the questions and the responses can be in a variety of media. Depending on the technical sophistication of the court reporter, the answers can be delivered in paper form, audiotape, videotape, computer files, or all of these forms. In cases involving extensive testimony, requesting and obtaining the response in electronic and computer form, as well as in paper form, can save the subsequent cost of adding the information to a litigation support system or to courtroom evidence management software.

Rule 32. Use of Depositions in Court Proceedings

(a) **Use of Depositions.** At the trial or upon the hearing of a motion or an interlocutory proceeding, any part or all of a deposition, so far as admissible under the rules of evidence applied as though the witness were then present and testifying, may be used against any party who was present or represented at the taking of the deposition or who had reasonable notice thereof, in accordance with any of the following provisions:

(1) Any deposition may be used by any party for the purpose of contradicting or impeaching the testimony of deponent as a witness, or for any other purpose permitted by the Federal Rules of Evidence.

(2) The deposition of a party or of anyone who at the time of taking the deposition was an officer, director, or managing agent, or a person designated under Rule 30(b)(6) or 31(a) to testify on behalf of a public or private corporation, partnership or association or governmental agency which is a party may be used by an adverse party for any purpose.

(3) The deposition of a witness, whether or not a party, may be used by any party for any purpose if the court finds:

(A) that the witness is dead; or

(B) that the witness is at a greater distance than 100 miles from the place of trial or hearing, or is out of the United States, unless it appears that the absence of the witness was procured by the party offering the deposition; or

(C) that the witness is unable to attend or testify because of age, illness, infirmity, or imprisonment; or

(D) that the party offering the deposition has been unable to procure the attendance of the witness by subpoena; or

(E) upon application and notice, that such exceptional circumstances exist as to make it desirable, in the interest of justice and with due regard to the importance of presenting the testimony of witnesses orally in open court, to allow the deposition to be used.

A deposition taken without leave of court pursuant to a notice under Rule 30 (a)(2)(C) shall not be used against a party who demonstrates that, when served with the notice, it was unable through the exercise of diligence to obtain counsel to represent it at the taking of the deposition; nor shall a deposition be used against a party who, having received less than 11 days notice of a deposition, has promptly upon receiving such notice filed a motion for a protective order under Rule 26(c)(2) requesting that the deposition not be held or be held at a different time or place and such motion is pending at the time the deposition is held.

(4) If only part of a deposition is offered in evidence by a party, an adverse party may require the offeror to introduce any other part which ought in fairness to be considered with the part introduced, and any party may introduce any other parts.

Substitution of parties pursuant to Rule 25 does not affect the right to use depositions previously taken; and when an action has been brought in any court of the United States or of any State and another action involving the same subject matter is afterward brought between the same parties or their representatives or successors in interest, all depositions lawfully taken and duly filed in the former action may be used in the latter as if originally taken therefor. A deposition previously taken may also be used as permitted by the Federal Rules of Evidence.

(b) Objections to Admissibility. Subject to the provisions of Rule 28(b) and subdivision (d)(3) of this rule, objection may be made at the trial or hearing to receiving in evidence any deposition or part thereof for any reason which would require the exclusion of the evidence if the witness were then present and testifying.

(c) Form of Presentation. Except as otherwise directed by the court, a party offering deposition testimony pursuant to this rule may offer it in stenographic or nonstenographic form, but, if in nonstenographic form, the party shall also provide the court with a transcript of the portions so offered. On request of any party in a case tried before a jury, deposition testimony offered other than for impeachment purposes shall be presented in nonstenographic form, if available, unless the court for good cause orders otherwise.

(d) Effect of Errors and Irregularities in Depositions.

(1) As to Notice. All errors and irregularities in the notice for taking a deposition are waived unless written objection is promptly served upon the party giving the notice.

(2) As to Disqualification of Officer. Objection to taking a deposition because of disqualification of the officer before whom it is to be taken is waived unless made before the taking of the deposition begins or as soon thereafter as the disqualification becomes known or could be discovered with reasonable diligence.

(3) As to Taking of Deposition.

(A) Objections to the competency of a witness or to the competency, relevancy, or materiality of testimony are not waived by failure to make them before or during the taking of the deposition, unless the ground of the objection is one which might have been obviated or removed if presented at that time.

(B) Errors and irregularities occurring at the oral examination in the manner of taking the deposition, in the form of the questions or answers, in the oath or affirmation, or in the conduct of parties, and errors of any kind which might be obviated, removed, or cured if promptly presented, are waived unless seasonable objection thereto is made at the taking of the deposition.

(C) Objections to the form of written questions submitted under Rule 31 are waived unless served in writing upon the party propounding them within the time allowed for serving the succeeding cross or other questions and within 5 days after service of the last questions authorized.

(4) As to Completion and Return of Deposition. Errors and irregularities in the manner in which the testimony is transcribed or the deposition is prepared, signed, certified, sealed, indorsed, transmitted, filed, or otherwise dealt with by the officer under Rules 30 and 31 are waived unless a motion to suppress the deposition or some part thereof is made with reasonable promptness after such defect is, or with due diligence might have been, ascertained.

Commentary

By David A. Sonenshein
Temple University Beasley School of Law

FRCP 32 governs the admissibility and use of depositions at trials and hearings. Assuming the deposition is offered against a party who was present at, represented at, or had notice of the deposition, the deposition may be used, so far as admissible under the Federal Rules of Evidence, as follows: (1) by any party for impeachment of the deponent as a witness or for any other purpose permitted by the Federal Rules of Evidence; (2) by an adverse party for any purpose (i.e., including the truth in lieu of live testimony) where the deponent is a party or was at the time of the deposition an officer, director, or managing agent, or FRCP 30(b)(6) designee which is a party; or (3) by any party for any purpose where the deponent is "unavailable" at the time of trial as defined in FRCP 32(a)(3)(A)–(D), or because of FRCP 32(a)(3)(E) "exceptional circumstances."

Note that the last paragraph of FRCP 32(a) provides an escape hatch against the use of depositions at trial where the party against whom it is offered demonstrates hardship in obtaining counsel or regarding the time and place of the deposition which existed at the time the deposition was held.

FRCP 32(a)(4) incorporates Fed.R.Evid. 106 and applies to depositions a "Rule of Completeness" treatment where a party offers only part of a deposition at a trial or hearing. This section of the Rule also permits the use of depositions against substituted parties and the use of depositions taken in a former action when used against a party or successor-in-interest in a later action under the same terms as set forth above.

Sections (b) and (d) of FRCP 32 govern objections to the admissibility of evidence contained in a deposition which is offered at a trial or hearing. If properly preserved during the deposition, objections are made at trial to deposition testimony for the same reasons they are made to testimony at trial. Objections to the competency of a witness, or the competency, relevance, or materiality or the hearsay nature of deposition testimony are not waived by failure to lodge such objections at the deposition unless the ground of the objection is one that could have been obviated upon a contemporaneous objection at the deposition. Objections to notice, errors, or irregularities in the taking of the deposition, or the qualification of the officer taking it, as well as objections to the form of the questions or answers or in the oath or affirmation will be waived at trial unless a contemporaneous objection was lodged at the deposition.

Note that FRCP 32 permits depositions to be offered at trial where the deposition is permitted by the terms of the Rule and is permitted by the Federal Rules of Evidence. Where the deposition is offered by the adversary of a party or the managing agent, director, or officer of a party, the deposition will be admissible under FRCP 32(a)(2) and will qualify as a party admission pursuant to Fed.R.Evid. 801(d).

Where the deposition is given by a nonparty witness, however, it will ordinarily qualify for admission under Fed.R.Evid. 804(b)(1) if it qualifies for admission under FRCP 32(a)(3). There may be occasions when all of the requirements of admissibility under Fed.R.Evid. 804(b)(1) may not be met (e.g., unavailability under FRE 804(a) or the party against whom the deposition is offered may have lacked the same motive to cross-examine at the deposition) even though the deposition qualifies for admission under FRCP 32(a)(3).

Rule 33. Interrogatories to Parties

(a) Availability. Without leave of court or written stipulation, any party may serve upon any other party written interrogatories, not exceeding 25 in number including all discrete subparts, to be answered by the party served or, if the party served is a public or private corporation or a partnership or association or governmental agency, by any officer or agent, who shall furnish such information as is available to the party. Leave to serve additional inter- rogatories shall be granted to the extent consistent with the principles of Rule 26(b)(2). Without leave of court or written stipulation, interrogatories may not be served before the time specified in Rule 26(d).

(b) Answers and Objections.

(1) Each interrogatory shall be answered separately and fully in writing under oath, unless it is objected to, in which event the objecting party shall state the reasons for objection and shall answer to the extent the interrogatory is not objectionable.

(2) The answers are to be signed by the person making them, and the objections signed by the attorney making them.

(3) The party upon whom the interrogatories have been served shall serve a copy of the answers, and objections if any, within 30 days after the service of the interrogatories. A shorter or longer time may be directed by the court or, in the absence of such an order, agreed to in writing by the parties subject to Rule 29.

(4) All grounds for an objection to an interrogatory shall be stated with specificity. Any ground not stated in a timely objection is waived unless the party's failure to object is excused by the court for good cause shown.

(5) The party submitting the interrogatories may move for an order under Rule 37(a) with respect to any objection to or other failure to answer an interrogatory.

(c) Scope; Use at Trial. Interrogatories may relate to any matters which can be inquired into under Rule 26(b)(1), and the answers may be used to the extent permitted by the rules of evidence.

An interrogatory otherwise proper is not necessarily objectionable merely because an answer to the interrogatory involves an opinion or contention that relates to fact or the application of law to fact, but the court may order that such an interrogatory need not be answered until after designated discovery has been completed or until a pre-trial conference or other later time.

(d) Option to Produce Business Records. Where the answer to an interrogatory may be derived or ascertained from the business records of the party upon whom the interrogatory has been served or from an examination, audit, or inspection of such business records, including a compilation, abstract, or summary thereof, and the burden of deriving or ascertaining the answer is substantially the same for the party serving the interrogatory as for the party served, it is a sufficient answer to such interrogatory to specify the records from which the answer may be derived or ascertained and to afford to the party serving the interrogatory reasonable opportunity to examine, audit, or inspect such records and to make copies, compilations, abstracts, or summaries. A specification shall be in sufficient detail to permit the interrogating party to locate and to identify, as readily as can the party served, the records from which the answer may be ascertained.

Commentary

By Shane Read
U.S. Attorney's Office, Northern District of Texas

Rule 33 provides that a party may serve upon any other party up to twenty-five written interrogatories (including all discrete subparts) which must be answered by the party served. Along with depositions, interrogatories are the bread and butter of civil litigation.

A party may not serve any party until after an initial attorney-scheduling meeting, required by FRCP 26(d), is held. Each interrogatory must be answered separately and under oath within 30 days after service. Evasive answers and qualified answers are prohibited; one should object if the question is unclear or beyond the proper scope of discovery. However, if a qualified answer is used to clarify the question and results in a forthright answer, such an answer is proper.

If there are objections, the objection must be specifically stated and the interrogatory must then be answered to the extent it is not objectionable. Blanket objections are improper, since each interrogatory must be answered separately. Objections are waived unless the grounds are stated in a timely manner, except where good cause can be shown for the failure to do so.

Where the answer to the interrogatory may be obtained from the party's business records and the burden is substantially the same for both parties, a party has the option to produce the records for examination from which the answer may be ascertained. The person making the answers must sign them under oath and the attorney must sign objections.

In most courts, interrogatories are used less often since the advent of FRCP 26(a)(1)–(3) which require much of the information previously obtained through the use of interrogatories (e.g., relevant witnesses, calculation of damages, insurance agreements, production of relevant documents, etc.). However, many districts have opted out of the requirements of Rule 26, making interrogatories an even more important tool in preparing one's case in those districts.

Interrogatories are efficient in determining an opposing party's factual contentions and obtaining precise answers regarding data that a deposition might not reveal. If a complaint is sufficient but nonetheless stated in general terms, one could propound "contention" interrogatories asking for the basis for a party's contention in particular paragraphs in a complaint. For example, if the plaintiff's complaint asserts that he was discriminated against on the basis of race, national origin, and sex and if the complaint details a factual basis for a claim based on race but not sex, the following interrogatory would be helpful: "State in full specific detail all facts which you contend support your allegation in paragraph ___ of Plaintiff's Original Complaint that ABC Company discriminated against Plaintiff on the basis of sex."

Such a "contention" interrogatory will help an attorney determine the germane legal issues, the strength of opposing side's contention, which documents should be examined, and which witnesses to interview. In short, interrogatories can be used to define the scope of the legal issues and facts presented in the lawsuit. An interrogatory is not objectionable simply because it asks for an opinion or contention that relates to fact or the application of law to fact.

Another effective way to use interrogatories is to ask for important dates, calculations of damages, and information that is derived from documents. The advantage here is that at a deposition, a deponent often does not remember exact figures, dates, etc. The interrogatory will ensure that such important information is timely provided and will avoid the delay and expense of having the deponent search through stacks of documents in order to answer the question at a deposition.

Interrogatories are also very important in determining other parties' lists of witnesses who may have relevant facts about a case. Such information is usually the springboard that starts the discovery process. Moreover, whatever the question, interrogatories are helpful because the opposing side has a continuing duty to supplement its answers, whether they relate to fact witnesses, damage calculations, etc., and such answers can be very damaging at a trial.

Assume, for example, that an employment discrimination case asserts retaliation and the plaintiff asked the defendant to describe how plaintiff's discipline compared with other similarly situated employees. In a rush to meet the answer deadline, the Company lists five employees from the regional office where plaintiff worked and their respective discipline. Typically, such an interrogatory is answered at the beginning of a lawsuit, years before a trial date is reached and well before the case is thoroughly investigated. At trial, if the defendant decides that instead of the five regional employees listed in its interrogatory, a more fair comparison would be to compare plaintiff's discipline to employees in all of its offices nationwide, the defendant would be bound by its unsupplemented answer in the interrogatory and prevented from asserting a full defense at trial.

Two obvious disadvantages to the use of interrogatories are that there is no chance to spontaneously follow-up on an answer as there would be in an oral deposition, and there is a limit, twenty-five including subparts, to the number of interrogatories a party may serve.

On that latter point, there is much confusion about what constitutes a legitimate subpart to an interrogatory so that it may count as one question. As long as the subparts ask for information related to the same topic, it is considered a single question. See *Kendall v. GES Exposition Services, Inc.*, (1997, DC Nev) 174 FRD 684.

For example, if the question asks "List all fact witnesses with relevant knowledge to the lawsuit" and the subparts provide for the witnesses' name, address, etc., then only one interrogatory has been propounded. However, if the question is a compound sentence, it will usually count as two interrogatories. For example, the following are improper: (1) "When did you first start having problems with your back and have you ever sought medical treatment for it?" and (2) "Please list any eyewitnesses to your alleged complaint of discrimination and describe where each witness was located and their relationship to you."

If one is on the receiving end of interrogatories, be alert to interrogatories that request the responding party to attach relevant documents to its responses. A novice might produce the document, but an alert party will object and force the requesting party to serve a request for production of documents.

Rule 34. Production of Documents and Things and Entry Upon Land for Inspection and Other Purposes

(a) Scope. Any party may serve on any other party a request (1) to produce and permit the party making the request, or someone acting on the requestor's behalf, to inspect and copy, any designated documents (including writings, drawings, graphs, charts, photographs, phonorecords, and other data compilations from which information can be obtained, translated, if necessary, by the respondent through detection devices into reasonably usable form), or to inspect and copy, test, or sample any tangible things which constitute or contain matters within the scope of Rule 26(b) and which are in the possession, custody or control of the party upon whom the request is served; or (2) to permit entry upon designated land or other property in the possession or control of the party upon whom the request is served for the purpose of inspection and measuring, surveying, photographing, testing, or sampling the property or any designated object or operation thereon, within the scope of Rule 26(b).

(b) Procedure. The request shall set forth, either by individual item or by category, the items to be inspected, and describe each with reasonable particularity. The request shall specify a reasonable time, place, and manner of making the inspection and performing the related acts. Without leave of court or written stipulation, a request may not be served before the time specified in Rule 26(d).

The party upon whom the request is served shall serve a written response within 30 days after the service of the request. A shorter or longer time may be directed by the court or, in the absence of such an order, agreed to in writing by the parties, subject to Rule 29. The response shall state, with respect to each item or category, that inspection and related activities will be permitted as requested, unless the request is objected to, in which event the reasons for the objection shall be stated. If objection is made to part of an item or category, the part shall be specified and inspection permitted of the remaining parts. The party submitting the request may move for an order under Rule 37(a) with respect to any objection to or other failure to respond to the request or any part thereof, or any failure to permit inspection as requested.

RULE 34. PRODUCTION OF DOCUMENTS AND THINGS AND ENTRY UPON LAND FOR INSPECTION AND OTHER PURPOSES

A party who produces documents for inspection shall produce them as they are kept in the usual course of business or shall organize and label them to correspond with the categories in the request.

(c) Persons Not Parties. A person not a party to the action may be compelled to produce documents and things or to submit to an inspection as provided in Rule 45.

Commentary

By Arnold S. Klein
Meltzer, Lippe, Goldstein & Schlissel

Federal Rule of Civil Procedure 34 is the primary discovery provision for obtaining documents, objects, and access to land from a party; though a subpoena pursuant to FRCP 45 may be used to gain access to documents, tangible things, or to permit the inspection of premises in the possession, custody, or control of a nonparty.

The purpose of the Rule is to make relevant and non-privileged documents and objects in the possession of one party available to the other, thus reducing surprise and permitting issues to be simplified and the trial to be expedited. See *Hickman v. Taylor*, 329 U.S. 495, 91 L. Ed. 451, 67 S. Ct. 385 (1947). Thus, FRCP 34, as part of an integrated scheme for the full disclosure of relevant information, is to be broadly and liberally construed. 7 Moore's Federal Practice, § 34.12 (2000). While discovery under FRCP 34 is most typically employed in pending civil actions, it is also available in some pre- and post-action proceedings, including proceedings to perpetuate testimony (FRCP 27(a)(3) and (b)) and to execute on a judgment (FRCP 69(a)).

Pursuant to FRCP 26(d), a FRCP 34 request may not be served before the parties have met and conferred pursuant to FRCP 26(f) unless the parties have stipulated otherwise, leave of court has been obtained, or earlier service is authorized under local rule. All FRCP 34 requests must describe with "reasonable particularity," by individual item or category, the items to be inspected. The goal of the "reasonable particularity" requirement is that a person of ordinary intelligence would know what documents must be produced, and that a court would be able to determine whether all requested documents have been produced. See *Mallinckrodt Chemical Works v. Goldman, Sachs & Co.*, 58 F.R.D. 348 (S.D.N.Y. 1973); *Camco, Inc. v. Baker Oil Tools, Inc.*, 45 F.R.D. 384 (S.D. Texas 1968). The request must also specify a "reasonable" time, place, and manner for the inspection and for performing the related acts. The time specified for the inspection must take into account the period specified in FRCP 34(b), within which the parties upon whom the request is served can serve a response to the request. While FRCP 34 requires requests to be in writing, it is not uncommon for litigants to make oral requests for documents at depositions. Such requests have been enforced, *Jackson v. Novell, Inc.*, 94 Civ. 3593 (MGC) (AJP), 1995 U.S. Dist. LEXIS 4162 (S.D.N.Y. 1995), but the better practice is to make such requests in writing and to confirm oral requests in writing. Oral requests cannot, however, be used to shorten the response time provided in FRCP 34(b). *Llewellyn v. North Am. Trading*, 93 Civ. 8894 (KMW), 1998 U.S. Dist. LEXIS 2555 (S.D.N.Y. 1998).

FRCP 34 broadly defines the items subject to a request for the production of documents. Designated documents sought by a request include "writings, drawings, graphs, charts, photographs, phonorecords and other data compilations from which information can be obtained, and translated, if necessary, by the respondent through detection devices into reasonably usable form." Local rules may supplement the definition of document as well as provide other uniform definitions and rules of construction for discovery requests. See, e.g., Local Civil FRCP 26.3 of the Southern and Eastern Districts of New York, which sets forth definitions and rules of construction that are deemed incorporated by reference into all discovery requests. It defines "document," for example, as "synonymous in meaning and equal in scope to the usage of this term in Federal Rule Civil Procedure 34(a), including, without limitation, electronic or computerized data compilations . . ." This local rule also provides that drafts or non-identical copies of documents (useful in finding relevant, and revealing, marginalia) must be produced. It is not uncommon for litigants to set forth these and other definitions or instructions in their FRCP 34 requests, including definitions of such terms as, "communications," "parties," "person," and "concerning." A local rule such as FRCP 26.3 of the Southern and Eastern Districts of New York can obviate the need to put several pages of such definitions and instructions in a FRCP 34 request.

In its language relating to the scope of a document request, it is significant that FRCP 34 uses the term "data compilation." Data compilation may include e-mail, telephone/voice mail messages, information stored on the hard drives of desktop and laptop computers, hand-held or personal digital assistants (e.g., Palm Pilots), computer disks, computer servers such as America Online, wide area networks such as the Internet, electronic archives, computers contained in appliances, and magnetic stripes on ATM and credit cards. Courts have consistently held that such electronic and computer items are discoverable. See, e.g., *Anti-Monopoly, Inc. v. Hasbro, Inc.*, 94 Civ. 2120 (LMM)(AJP), 1995 U.S. Dist. LEXIS 16355 (S.D.N.Y. 1995) ("... today it is black letter law that computer data is discoverable if relevant"), citing *Santiago v. Miles*, 121 F.R.D. 636, 640, 1988 U. S. Dist. LEXIS 9363 (S.D.N.Y. 1988) (a request for raw information in computer files is proper and the information is obtainable under the discovery rules). See also Federal Rules of Civil Procedure Advisory Committee Notes, 1970 Amendment, stating that the Rule is applicable to computer information (and also stating, subject to conditions that may be imposed by the court, "... that when the data can as a practical matter be made usable by the discovering party only through respondent's devices, respondent may be required to use his devices to translate the data into usable form").

Because an increasing amount of discoverable information is never printed on paper, understanding the kind of computer information available, where to look for it, and how to get it is all-important. Indeed, in order to facilitate the discovery of electronic information, hiring a computer expert to perform the actual computer discovery may be a necessity. Such an expert must have the skills and tools to carry out the discovery effectively and can also assist in drafting discovery demands to ensure that all relevant computer data is requested.

During the course of discovery the litigants should, among other things, identify the type of computer systems used by their adversary. They should also learn how it operates, how information is created, transmitted, stored, used, retrieved, preserved, destroyed, and where such information is located. In addition to the obvious networked computers and the stand-alone computers in a party's facilities, it may be useful to include laptop computers and home computers of key employees in the set of systems and equipment covered by the request.

Attorneys may receive requests for "ghost data" (deleted materials still lurking in the computer system); "metadata" (information as to the modification of a file); "legacy data" (older files that cannot be accessed by current systems); and other newly evolved categories of data. Before agreeing to provide the requested information, attorneys should fully understand what is being requested.

Deleted material, for example, is a potentially fertile area for disagreement. While there is no agreement, several experts have suggested that deleted material (e-mails, digital voice mail, etc.) should be afforded the same status as shredded documents and should not be discoverable. The history of changes to a file as well as discarded drafts can lead to embarrassing situations if one is not aware of the changes to key documents, when the changes occurred, and the reasons why.

And agreeing to provide materials from an obsolete system can cost one's client significant time and money. If one fully understands what is requested, then one can better utilize FRCP 26(b)(2) to limit the request.

E-mail is a particularly difficult area. Replies to e-mails and retransmitted e-mail can be a rich source of information (electronic marginalia), but can be an almost open-ended process. One might consider requesting network logs to find e-mails that were forwarded to unauthorized recipients or sent to "blind copy" recipients. It is difficult to fully anticipate both the necessary scope and the practical limitations of requests for electronic data, and it is very useful to obtain the advice of an expert both in responding to requests for e-mails and in preparing requests.

Requests for documents should include standards to ensure readability (visually and electronically) and completeness. When large numbers of documents are duplicated, the quality may suffer and poring over barely legible material can take its toll both as to accuracy and cost. Similarly, standards should be stated when the documents are going to be scanned and converted to searchable data files. Receiving low-quality images, third-generation copies, or "dirty" documents (whether by accident or by design) can significantly increase the cost of setting up searchable data files and the overall cost of litigation.

One should consider requesting that documents be delivered in electronic media (e.g., document images on a CD or DVD), particularly if there are several parties involved. While the cost of the initial set of document copies is higher, the costs for subsequent copies are much lower and the quality much better. Moreover, depositions and other transcribed materials are increasingly available in computer searchable form, either from an electronic file produced by the recorder or through voice recognition techniques. Anticipating use of computer transcripts or computer files and exhibits at trial may require capturing data in electronic form in the discovery stage in order to effectively manage overall costs.

Few cases have the document volume or the cost justification to warrant use of a full-scale electronic document management system, but as costs come down and the document capture and management tools—plus expertise—become more cost-effective, they will become more widespread. If an electronic document management system is to be used, the expertise necessary to utilize the system should be obtained as soon as possible, either from one's own IT department or from quality outside experts (be very careful if a client suggests using their IT capability for anything other than basic data or document capture). If one is using an electronic document management system, care should be taken that privileged files are not mingled (or appear to be mingled) with those of an expert for fear of losing privileged characterization of the file.

The documents and tangible things that are the subject of a FRCP 34 request must be in the "possession, custody or control" of the party upon whom the request is served. When entry upon designated land or other property is sought, it must be in the "possession or control" of the party served. Parties have possession, custody, or control of a document if they have the legal right to obtain it. See, e.g., *MTB Bank v. Federal Armored Express, Inc.*, 93 Civ. 5594 (LBS), 1998 U.S. Dist. LEXIS 922 (S.D.N.Y. 1998) (documents in possession of party's current or former counsel deemed to be within party's possession, custody and control); *Bank of New York v. Meridien Biao Bank Tanzania Ltd.*, 171 F.R.D. 135, 154 (S.D.N.Y. 1997) (documents in the physical possession of defendant's accountants held to be within custody and control of defendant because defendant had the legal right to obtain them). See, generally, *Gerling Int'l Ins. Co. v. Commissioner*, 839 F.2d 131, 140–41 (3d Civ. 1988) (discussing control by corporations over documents in possession of parent, subsidiary or sister entities). Even if a document is located beyond the territorial jurisdiction of the court, a party must produce it if it is determined to be in the party's possession, custody, or control. *Dietrich v. Bauer*, 95 Civ. 7051 (RWS), 2000 U.S. Dist. LEXIS 11729 (S.D.N.Y. 2000) (documents in the possession of defendant's foreign affiliate were discoverable even though the documents in question were outside of the court's jurisdiction).

The requesting parties or their attorney must sign all FRCP 34 requests according to the certification requirements of FRCP 26(g). Once a request has been served, the parties have thirty days to respond to it unless the court orders or the parties stipulate otherwise. If the responding parties fail to respond to the demand, the parties seeking discovery may move under FRCP 37(a) to compel discovery and for appropriate sanctions. At a minimum, the parties' response must state, as to each item or category, that the inspection and related activities will be permitted as requested, or is objected to, or that the items or categories do not exist or are not in their possession, custody, or control.

If the responding parties object to certain demands, FRCP 34(b) requires those parties to state their objections and the reasons for them. If an objection is made to part of an item or category, that part must be specified, and inspection of the remaining parts must be permitted. The grounds upon which a party may object to the production of documents include: (1) the documents requested contain information that is privileged or protected under the work product doctrine; (2) responding to the request would be unduly burdensome; (3) the request is vague and ambiguous; and (4) the documents requested are irrelevant to the subject matter involved in the pending action. The responding parties and their attorney are also subject to the signing requirements of FRCP 26(g).

If the parties object to any request on the grounds of privilege or work product, they must expressly set forth their claim of privilege or work product in a privilege log. That privilege log must describe the nature of the documents, communications, or things not produced or disclosed in sufficient detail such that, without revealing privileged or protected information, it will enable other parties and the court to assess the applicability of the privilege or protection claimed. Local court rules may also specify additional requirements for a privilege log. See, e.g., Local Civil FRCP 26.2 for the Eastern and Southern Districts of New York, which sets out the specific information that must be provided when a privilege is asserted. Failure to provide a privilege log may result in the waiver of any privilege claims. See, e.g., *A.I.A. Holdings, S.A. v. Lehman Brothers, Inc.*, 97 Civ. 4978 (LMM) (HBP), 2000 U.S. Dist. LEXIS 15141 (S.D.N.Y. 2000).

From the perspective of the party demanding discovery, efforts should be made to maximize the value of a privilege log because withheld documents may prove to be the "smoking gun" in a case or reveal clues to other discoverable information. This can be done by: (1) demanding a log containing (a) the type of document, the document's date, and number of pages, (b) the basis for withholding the document, (c) the author and recipient of the document, persons copied on the document, and the custodian of the document, (d) the subject matter and purpose of the document, (e) date of the document, and (f) the production numbers, if any, on the document; (2) obtaining a case management or discovery order specifying (a) the information that must be contained in the log, (b) a deadline for the production of the log, (c) sanctions that will be imposed if the order is violated, and (d) that the privilege or work product claim will be waived if such information is not provided; and (3) obtaining a privilege log early in the case so that crucial documents may be used effectively in the litigation.

Documents that are produced must be produced "as they are kept in the usual course of business," or they must be organized and labeled to correspond to the categories of items specified in the request. The provision on the procedure for producing documents was added to FRCP 34(b) in order to avoid the deliberate mixing and obscuring of critical documents. Federal Rules of Civil Procedure Advisory Committee Notes, 1980 amendment. In this vein, responding parties opting to produce documents that are kept in the usual course of business cannot just dump thousands of unorganized documents on an adversary. They must produce documents that are sufficiently organized and of sufficient quality that the requesting party can make reasonable use of them. See, e.g., *Standard Dyeing and Finishing Co. v. Arma Textile Printers Corp.*, 85 Civ. 5399 (CSH), 1987 U.S. Dist. LEXIS 868 (S.D.N.Y. 1987); 7 Moore's § 34.14(3)(c) (2000).

Anticipate what resources are required to deal with the requested material. Analyzing large volumes of hard copy or electronic materials requires that one have the tools and the experts to deal with the materials. While most discovery disputes involve a party's reluctance to surrender information, in certain cases a party demanding discovery should anticipate what would happen if the requested party responded fully and vigorously. If one anticipates a large package of documents in the mail but instead receives a truckload of documents at the back door, the entire cost basis of the case can become untenable. Although difficult, it is useful to identify an estimated volume of data, and request to be notified if the volume substantially exceeds that estimate.

Rule 35. Physical and Mental Examination of Persons

(a) Order for Examination. When the mental or physical condition (including the blood group) of a party or of a person in the custody or under the legal control of a party, is in controversy, the court in which the action is pending may order the party to submit to a physical or mental examination by a suitably licensed or certified examiner or to produce for examination the person in the party's custody or legal control. The order may be made only on motion for good cause shown and upon notice to the person to be examined and to all parties and shall specify the time, place, manner, conditions, and scope of the examination and the person or persons by whom it is to be made.

(b) Report of Examiner.

(1) If requested by the party against whom an order is made under Rule 35(a) or the person examined, the party causing the examination to be made shall deliver to the requesting party a copy of the detailed written report of the examiner setting out the examiner's findings, including results of all tests made, diagnoses and conclusions, together with like reports of all earlier examinations of the same condition. After delivery the party causing the examination shall be entitled upon request to receive from the party against whom the order is made a like report of any examination, previously or thereafter made, of the same condition, unless, in the case of a report of examination of a person not a party, the party shows that the party is unable to obtain it. The court on motion may make an order against a party requiring delivery of a report on such terms as are just, and if an examiner fails or refuses to make a report the court may exclude the examiner's testimony if offered at trial.

(2) By requesting and obtaining a report of the examination so ordered or by taking the deposition of the examiner, the party examined waives any privilege the party may have in that action or any other involving the same controversy, regarding the testimony of every other person who has examined or may thereafter examine the party in respect of the same mental or physical condition.

(3) This subdivision applies to examinations made by agreement of the parties, unless the agreement expressly provides otherwise. This subdivision does not preclude discovery of a report of an examiner or the taking of a deposition of the examiner in accordance with the provisions of any other rule.

(c) Definitions. For the purpose of this rule, a psychologist is a psychologist licensed or certified by a State or the District of Columbia.

Commentary

By G. Leroy Street
The Street Law Firm

Rule 35(a) allows a party to seek a court-ordered physical or mental examination of another party (or a represented person) from the court in which the action is pending. The movant must show that the particular condition for which examination is sought is "in controversy" and that "good cause" exists for ordering the examination. These requirements are not simple formalities. The movant cannot prevail based on conclusory allegations in pleadings nor the mere relevance of the anticipated evidence to the case. *Schlagenhauf v. Holder*, 379 U.S. 104, 13 L. Ed. 2d 152, 85 S. Ct. 234 (1964).

While the Rule is to be construed liberally in favor of discovery, it is not intended to authorize a sweeping medical or psychological examination. It is intended to level the playing field between parties in their respective efforts to appraise a specific medical condition. Whether to order an examination, and the extent of any examination, is committed to the discretion of the court.

A physical condition normally is "in controversy" if it constitutes the alleged injury suffered. An emotional condition typically is deemed to be "in controversy" only if there is: (1) the assertion of a specific cause of action for intentional or negligent infliction of emotional distress, (2) an allegation of a specific mental or psychiatric injury or disorder, (3) a claim of unusually severe emotional distress, (4) a proffer of expert testimony in support of the claim, or (5) an admission that the mental condition is in controversy.

RULE 35. PHYSICAL AND MENTAL EXAMINATION
OF PERSONS

"Good cause" usually requires a showing of a need for the information sought and a lack of means for obtaining the information elsewhere. *Acosta v. Tenneco Oil Co.*, 913 F.2d 205 (5th Cir. 1990).

The court may decide a request on affidavits and discovery products without a hearing. Thus, the prudent movant will attach discovery responses to the motion to establish the "in controversy" element. "Good cause" will be shown by an expert's affidavit showing that existing material is inadequate to evaluate the condition and that the requested examination is necessary to make the evaluation.

If appropriate, the party opposing the requested examination should controvert the movant's evidence on the issues of "good cause" and "in controversy." In addition, the non-movant may contest the validity of the proposed test or show that it would unreasonably jeopardize the well-being of the examinee. Since the order for an examination must state the time, place, manner, conditions and scope of the examination, the opposing party also may seek limitations on these matters (e.g., an expert in one field may be precluded from undertaking tests relevant only to expression of opinions in other fields of expertise).

It is left to the court's discretion whether an attorney or other third person may be present during an examination. However, unless the examiner proposes to use unorthodox or potentially harmful techniques, third-party observers are normally excluded based on possible contamination of the process. If a third-party is permitted to be present, the court may impose restrictions on the actions of the third-party during the examination. Recording devices are sometimes permitted.

The bias of a proposed examiner ordinarily must be handled by cross-examination at trial. Therefore, opposing a Rule 35 motion on this ground is ill-conceived unless there is some evidence that the examiner will begin the examination with a preconceived belief regarding the condition of the particular person to be examined.

The court's order must identify the examiner, who need not be a doctor, but is to be "suitably licensed or certified." This suitability requirement reconfirms the court's general "gatekeeper" role regarding use of experts. Nevertheless, the Rule contemplates that normally the movant will propose an examiner, the person to be examined will raise any valid objection, and absent objection the court will appoint the movant's proposed examiner. Once the examiner is appointed, no party should communicate with the examiner without court approval other than to arrange the appointment and to arrange payment of fees.

Rule 35(b) requires that upon request the movant will provide a "detailed written report" to the person examined. By making this request, the examined person waives any privilege attached to other examinations of the same condition. Once this request is made, all reports on the condition in question in the possession of either the movant or the person examined, regardless of when made, must be exchanged upon request. The report requirements are automatically incorporated in an agreed examination unless the agreement provides otherwise.

Rule 36. Requests for Admission

(a) Request for Admission. A party may serve upon any other party a written request for the admission, for purposes of the pending action only, of the truth of any matters within the scope of Rule 26(b)(1) set forth in the request that relate to statements or opinions of fact or of the application of law to fact, including the genuineness of any documents described in the request. Copies of documents shall be served with the request unless they have been or are otherwise furnished or made available for inspection and copying. Without leave of court or written stipulation, requests for admission may not be served before the time specified in Rule 26(d).

Each matter of which an admission is requested shall be separately set forth. The matter is admitted unless, within 30 days after service of the request, or within such shorter or longer time as the court may allow or as the parties may agree to in writing, subject to Rule 29, the party to whom the request is directed serves upon the party requesting the admission a written answer or objection addressed to the matter, signed by the party or by the party's attorney. If objection is made, the reasons therefor shall be stated. The answer shall specifically deny the matter or set forth in detail the reasons why the answering party cannot truthfully admit or deny the matter. A denial shall fairly meet the substance of the requested admission, and when good faith requires that a party qualify an answer or deny only a part of the matter of which an admission is requested, the party shall specify so much of it as is true and qualify or deny the remainder. An answering party may not give lack of information or knowledge as a reason for failure to admit or deny unless the party states that the party has made reasonable inquiry and that the information known or readily obtainable by the party is insufficient to enable the party to admit or deny. A party who considers that a matter of which an admission has been requested presents a genuine issue for trial may not, on that ground alone, object to the request; the party may, subject to the provisions of Rule 37(c), deny the matter or set forth reasons why the party cannot admit or deny it.

The party who has requested the admissions may move to determine the sufficiency of the answers or objections. Unless the court determines that an objection is justified, it shall order that an answer be served. If the court determines that an answer does not comply with the requirements of this rule, it may order either that the matter is admitted or that an amended answer be served. The court may, in lieu of these orders, determine that final disposition of the request be made at a pre-trial conference or at a designated time prior to trial. The provisions of Rule 37(a)(4) apply to the award of expenses incurred in relation to the motion.

(b) Effect of Admission. Any matter admitted under this rule is conclusively established unless the court on motion permits withdrawal or amendment of the admission. Subject to the provision of Rule 16 governing amendment of a pre-trial order, the court may permit withdrawal or amendment when the presentation of the merits of the action will be subserved thereby and the party who obtained the admission fails to satisfy the court that withdrawal or amendment will prejudice that party in maintaining the action or defense on the merits. Any admission made by a party under this rule is for the purpose of the pending action only and is not an admission for any other purpose nor may it be used against the party in any other proceeding.

Commentary

By Mark D. Risk
D'Agostino, Levine & Landesman

FRCP 36 permits a party to seek admissions of specific matters of fact, opinions of fact, or the application of law to fact, including the genuineness of specific documents and use those admissions at trial. A properly served, written FRCP 36 request must be responded to within 30 days or such other period as may be mutually agreed upon by the parties. A request for admissions may be used at any time within the time allowed by the court for discovery. These admissions are for the purposes of the pending action only.

FRCP 36 provides a means to reduce the scope of both discovery and trial by compelling an opponent to admit during discovery matters that would otherwise have to be proven at trial.

An FRCP 36 request must specifically set forth each point on which an admission is sought. These points should be set out as declarative statements on which admissions are sought, e.g., as "true or false" questions. One should state each proposition on which an admission is sought as simply as possible, using one fact per question. One should break up complex questions into subparts, so that one can isolate the specific issue that is not admitted, and obtain admissions as to everything else.

Be very clear in each request. Your adversary is looking for opportunities to avoid making admissions where not absolutely necessary, so edit your requests carefully to remove fuzziness and loopholes. Your FRCP 36 request should sound like a series of good cross-examination questions—the shorter and simpler the proposition, the more difficult it is for the responding party to wriggle out of an admission due to a claimed defect or ambiguity in the question.

FRCP 36 requests are often used in connection with documents. These requests are to establish by admission the genuineness of specific documents (or of any other element of the evidentiary foundation required for their admission at trial, such as the elements of a particular exception to the hearsay rule). FRCP 36 requires that you attach to the request any documents that are the subject of the request, unless they have been produced in discovery. As more federal courts impose time limits on depositions, FRCP 36 requests concerning documents will become more important discovery options because they save time.

The responding party is required to admit those matters that it knows are true; to make a specific denial; or to explain in detail the reasons that it cannot truthfully admit or deny. FRCP 36(a) imposes strict responsibilities on the responding party. Any individual request not responded to within the time allowed is deemed admitted in the lawsuit as against the non-responding party.

The responding party may object to a specific request, but must set forth the reasons for the objection. A denial of a particular matter must address the substance of the request, and the responding party may not be permitted to deny an entire requested admission where it can in good faith limit its denial to a part of the proposition on which the admission is sought. The responding party may not decline to admit a particular matter based on lack of information or knowledge, unless it states that it has made reasonable inquiry, and that the information known or readily obtainable is not sufficient to enable it either to deny or admit the matter. Either the party or the attorney must sign the response to the FRCP 36 request.

The court may make a post-trial award of economic sanctions, including attorney fees, if a party fails to admit the truth of a matter, or the genuineness of a document that is proved to be true or genuine at trial. FRCP 37(c)(2).

FRCP 36 permits the requesting party to seek the court's assistance if it believes that any of the responses are defective. (The responding party also has the option of making a motion for a protective order under FRCP 26(b) in order to obtain a ruling on any of the specific requests.) If the court determines that an objection to a specific request is not justified, it must direct that the party provide an answer to the request. The court may require service of an amended answer, or may simply deem the matter at issue admitted. The court's power to award sanctions for improper conduct of discovery under FRCP 37 applies to FRCP 36 responses. As a requesting attorney, be willing to go to the court to compel your adversary to give proper responses, but use discretion. Try to resolve differences with your adversary first, document those efforts, and prioritize the issues that you bring to the court.

It is poor practice for a responding party to find cute, hyper-technical reasons to deny propositions that are in substance truthful. Ethical obligations and the threat of sanctions aside, the loss of credibility with the court that results from being forced to explain a questionable denial to a judge or magistrate judge will probably do more damage to both attorney and client than the admission of the fact at issue.

RULE 36. REQUESTS FOR ADMISSION

An admission under FRCP 36 is similar in effect to a stipulation or an admission in a pleading. Any matter admitted in a response to an FRCP 36 request is "conclusively established" within the pending lawsuit as against the admitting party, but is of no effect and may not be used in any other action. By motion, a party may seek permission to withdraw or amend an admission previously given. The court may grant such relief as long as the party who obtained the admission is not prejudiced by the granting of the motion, e.g., a party may be prejudiced where its reliance on the admission caused it not to seek other means to prove the proposition at issue.

Rule 37. Failure to Make Disclosure or Cooperate in Discovery; Sanctions

(a) Motion for Order Compelling Disclosure or Discovery. A party, upon reasonable notice to other parties and all persons affected thereby, may apply for an order compelling disclo- sure or discovery as follows:

(1) Appropriate Court. An application for an order to a party shall be made to the court in which the action is pending. An application for an order to a person who is not a party shall be made to the court in the district where the discovery is being, or is to be, taken.

(2) Motion.

(A) If a party fails to make a disclosure required by Rule 26(a), any other party may move to compel disclosure and for appropriate sanctions. The motion must include a certification that the movant has in good faith conferred or attempted to confer with the party not making the disclosure in an effort to secure the disclosure without court action.

(B) If a deponent fails to answer a question propounded or submitted under Rules 30 or 31, or a corporation or other entity fails to make a designation under Rule 30(b)(6) or 31(a), or a party fails to answer an interrogatory submitted under Rule 33, or if a party, in response to a request for inspection submitted under Rule 34, fails to respond that inspection will be permitted as requested or fails to permit inspection as requested, the discovering party may move for an order compelling answer, or a designation, or an order compelling inspection in accordance with the request. The motion must include a certification that the movant has in good faith conferred or attempted to confer with the person or party failing to make the discovery in an effort to secure the information or material without court action. When taking a deposition on oral examination, the proponent of the question may complete or adjourn the examination before applying for an order.

RULE 37. FAILURE TO MAKE DISCLOSURE OR COOPERATE IN DISCOVERY; SANCTIONS

(3) Evasive or Incomplete Disclosure, Answer, or Response. For purposes of this subdivision an evasive or incomplete disclosure, answer, or response is to be treated as a failure to disclose, answer, or respond.

(4) Expenses and Sanctions.

(A) If the motion is granted or if the disclosure or requested discovery is provided after the motion was filed, the court shall, after affording an opportunity to be heard, require the party or deponent whose conduct necessitated the motion or the party or attorney advising such conduct or both of them to pay to the moving party the reasonable expenses incurred in making the motion, including attorney's fees, unless the court finds that the motion was filed without the movant's first making a good faith effort to obtain the disclosure or discovery without court action, or that the opposing party's nondisclosure, response, or objection was substantially justified, or that other circumstances make an award of expenses unjust.

(B) If the motion is denied, the court may enter any protective order authorized under Rule 26(c) and shall, after affording an opportunity to be heard, require the moving party or the attorney filing the motion or both of them to pay to the party or deponent who opposed the motion the reasonable expenses incurred in opposing the motion, including attorney's fees, unless the court finds that the making of the motion was substantially justified or that other circumstances make an award of expenses unjust.

(C) If the motion is granted in part and denied in part, the court may enter any protective order authorized under Rule 26(c) and may, after affording an opportunity to be heard, apportion the reasonable expenses incurred in relation to the motion among the parties and persons in a just manner.

(b) Failure to comply with order.

(1) Sanctions by Court in District Where Deposition Is Taken. If a deponent fails to be sworn or to answer a question after being directed to do so by the court in the district in which the deposition is being taken, the failure may be considered a contempt of that court.

(2) Sanctions by Court in Which Action Is Pending. If a party or an officer, director, or managing agent of a party or a person designated under Rule 30(b)(6) or 31(a) to testify on behalf of a party fails to obey an order to provide or permit discovery, including an order made under subdivision (a) of this rule or Rule 35, or if a party fails to obey an order entered under Rule 26(f), the court in which the action is pending may make such orders in regard to the failure as are just, and among others the following:

(A) An order that the matters regarding which the order was made or any other designated facts shall be taken to be established for the purposes of the action in accordance with the claim of the party obtaining the order;

(B) An order refusing to allow the disobedient party to support or oppose designated claims or defenses, or prohibiting that party from introducing designated matters in evidence;

(C) An order striking out pleadings or parts thereof, or staying further proceedings until the order is obeyed, or dismissing the action or proceeding or any part thereof, or rendering a judgment by default against the disobedient party;

(D) In lieu of any of the foregoing orders or in addition thereto, an order treating as a contempt of court the failure to obey any orders except an order to submit to a physical or mental examination;

(E) Where a party has failed to comply with an order under Rule 35(a) requiring that party to produce another for examination, such orders as are listed in paragraphs (A), (B), and (C) of this subdivision, unless the party failing to comply shows that that party is unable to produce such person for examination.

In lieu of any of the foregoing orders or in addition thereto, the court shall require the party failing to obey the order or the attorney advising that party or both to pay the reasonable expenses, including attorney's fees, caused by the failure, unless the court finds that the failure was substantially justified or that other circumstances make an award of expenses unjust.

(c) Failure to Disclose; False or Misleading Disclosure; Refusal to Admit.

(1) A party that without substantial justification fails to disclose information required by Rule 26(a) or 26(e)(1), or to amend a prior response to discovery as required by Rule 26(e)(2), is not, unless such failure is harmless, permitted to use as evidence at a trial, at a hearing, or on a motion any witness or information not so disclosed. In addition to or in lieu of this sanction, the court, on motion and after affording an opportunity to be heard, may impose other appropriate sanctions. In addition to requiring payment of reasonable expenses, including attorney's fees, caused by the failure, these sanctions may include any of the actions authorized under Rule 37(b)(2)(A), (B), and (C) and may include informing the jury of the failure to make the disclosure.

(2) If a party fails to admit the genuineness of any document or the truth of any matter as requested under Rule 36, and if the party requesting the admissions thereafter proves the genuineness of the document or the truth of the matter, the requesting party may apply to the court for an order requiring the other party to pay the reasonable expenses incurred in making that proof, including reasonable attorney's fees. The court shall make the order unless it finds that (A) the request was held objectionable pursuant to Rule 36(a), or (B) the admission sought was of no substantial importance, or (C) the party failing to admit had reasonable ground to believe that the party might prevail on the matter, or (D) there was other good reason for the failure to admit.

(d) Failure of Party to Attend at Own Deposition or Serve Answers to Interrogatories or Respond to Request for Inspection. If a party or an officer, director, or managing agent of a party or a person designated under Rule 30(b)(6) or 31(a) to testify on behalf of a party fails (1) to appear before the officer who is to take the deposition, after being served with a proper notice, or (2) to serve answers or objections to interrogatories submitted under Rule 33, after proper service of the interrogatories, or (3) to serve a written response to a request for inspection submitted under Rule 34, after proper service of the request, the court in which the action is pending on motion may make such orders in regard to the failure as are just, and among others it may take any action authorized under subparagraphs (A), (B), and (C) of subdivision (b)(2) of this rule. Any motion specifying a failure under clause (2) or (3) of this subdivision shall include a certification that the movant has in good faith conferred or attempted to confer with the party failing to answer or respond in an effort to obtain such answer or response without court action. In lieu of any order or in addition thereto, the court shall require the party failing to act or the attorney advising that party or both to pay the reasonable expenses, including attorney's fees, caused by the failure unless the court finds that the failure was substantially justified or that other circumstances make an award of expenses unjust.

The failure to act described in this subdivision may not be excused on the ground that the discovery sought is objectionable unless the party failing to act has a pending motion for a protective order as provided by Rule 26(c).

(e) [Abrogated]

(f) [Repealed]

(g) Failure to Participate in the Framing of a Discovery Plan. If a party or a party's attorney fails to participate in the development and submission of a proposed discovery plan as required by Rule 26(f), the court may, after opportunity for hearing, require such party or attorney to pay to any other party the reasonable expenses, including attorney's fees, caused by the failure.

Commentary

By Mark D. Risk
D'Agostino, Levine & Landesman

FRCP 37 provides the court with a variety of remedies to address a party's failure to comply with discovery obligations. The

RULE 37. FAILURE TO MAKE DISCLOSURE OR COOPERATE IN DISCOVERY; SANCTIONS

Rule emphasizes the availability of economic sanctions, including reimbursement of the other party's attorney's fees resulting from the wrongful discovery conduct.

FRCP 37 can be misleading to the inexperienced litigator because its long catalog of objectionable discovery practices and its rich menu of remedies fosters the misimpression that federal courts are eager to punish the offenders in routine discovery disputes. Think of FRCP 37 as a tool; by establishing a set of rules and penalties for discovery abuses, it assists a party attempting to resolve its discovery problems with its adversary. The sanctions and other harsh remedies are generally reserved for those who act in bad faith.

FRCP 37(a) provides that a party may apply for an order to compel discovery and for sanctions against the opponent. Before making the motion, the movant must attempt to confer in good faith with the party or person against whom the motion is directed, in an effort to obtain the disclosure without judicial intervention, and include a certification specifically setting forth those efforts as part of the motion.

An FRCP 37 motion may be made with respect to the conduct of a nonparty from whom discovery has been sought by subpoena. Where the person or entity resides in another part of the country, the motion to compel discovery may need to be made in the federal district court for the district in which the nonparty resides. FRCP 37(a)(1); see also FRCP 45. That federal district court may transfer any motions for resolution by the court in which the action is pending, see *In re Digital Equipment Corp.*, 949 F.2d 228, 231 (8th Cir. 1991), or stay proceedings on the motion pending guidance from the court in which the action is pending. See *In re Sealed Case*, 141 F.3d 337, 343 (D.C. Cir. 1998).

FRCP 37(a) sets forth a wide variety of specific failures that might be the basis for an FRCP 37 motion: failure by a party to make the voluntary initial disclosures required by FRCP 26(a), failure to answer a question at an oral or written deposition, failure to designate a corporate representative for deposition testimony, failure to answer an interrogatory, and failure to respond to a FRCP 34 request for an inspection. Evasive or incomplete disclosure, such as the artificially restrictive or hypertechnical construction of discovery requests to avoid production of information, is a proper basis for a sanctions motion. FRCP 37(a)(3).

The lawyer seeking discovery must keep in mind that an adversary asserting a reasonable position in good faith will probably will not be sanctioned. The requesting lawyer should make a record of his efforts to confer with the adversary, conducting the discussions by letter or using letters to memorialize telephone negotiations. One should prepare the documentation bearing in mind that it will be attached to motion papers and read by a judge. The lawyer seeking discovery should be the one who states the positions clearly and calmly, cites authority, and refrains from silly threats. It may be appropriate to remind your adversary of his obligations under the federal rules and your right to seek FRCP 37 sanctions, but do it professionally—discovery disputes often have no established answer, and the winner may be the side that presents its position most sensibly.

FRCP 37(a)(4) sets forth the court's powers in connection with a motion to compel discovery and award sanctions. At first glance it is written in a manner that appears to encourage the court to award sanctions, but it also erects procedural and substantive hurdles to the moving party.

If the court grants the motion, or if the discovery sought by the motion is provided after the motion is filed, the court then considers the request for sanctions. It must first give the party or person opposing the motion an additional opportunity to be heard, by oral argument and/or written submission, on the sanctions request. FRCP 37 provides that the court "shall" direct either the person against which the motion was made or the party or attorney who advised its conduct, or both, to pay the moving party's reasonable expenses in connection with the motion including attorney's fees.

The court may decline to award the sanctions, however, if the motion was made without the movant's making a prior good faith effort to obtain the discovery without judicial intervention, or if the opposing party's conduct is "substantially justified," or that the award of the expenses would be unjust. The Supreme Court has stated that the conduct meets the "substantially justified" standard when there is a genuine dispute about which reasonable lawyers could legitimately disagree. *Pierce v. Underwood*, 487 U.S. 552, 101 L. Ed. 2d 490, 108 S. Ct. 2541 (1988). The "substantially justified" standard swallows the Rule—the court will not award sanctions in the typical discovery dispute between lawyers who assert good faith objections to discovery requests.

There is an additional reason for the party seeking discovery to proceed cautiously. One of the ironies of discovery sanctions under FRCP 37 is that they can be awarded for misuse of FRCP 37 itself. If the court denies the motion to compel the discovery, it must require the moving party (or the attorney who filed the motion, or both) to pay the reasonable expenses, including attorney fees, incurred by the party or nonparty in opposing the motion. The court may decline to award the sanctions if the motion was substantially justified or an award of expenses would be unjust. If the motion is granted in part, the court may apportion the reasonable expenses among the parties (and nonparties and attorneys).

The party against whom the discovery is sought should not take comfort in the obstacles to sanctions imposed by FRCP 37. A federal discovery request is a serious matter, and the rules favor free and open discovery. A federal judge may be extremely impatient with a party's efforts to impede its adversary's discovery. Attempt in good faith to resolve disputes with your adversary, make offers of compromise, and document those efforts in correspondence with your adversary.

In the event an FRCP 37 motion is filed against you, you will want to be able to demonstrate that you have asserted reasonable positions in a professional manner, and attempted in good faith to find solutions to the problems.

FRCP 37(b) sets forth the sanctions for certain failures to obey court orders regarding discovery. FRCP 37 has been amended to make clear that it is intended to apply to all manner of discovery orders.

The remedy of contempt of court is available where a deponent fails to answer a question after being ordered to do so. FRCP 37(b)(1). For other failures, the court has a menu of remedial options, including treating facts which were the object of the discovery as established in the lawsuit; prohibiting the disobedient party from supporting or opposing certain claims or introducing certain matters into evidence or striking parts of its pleadings; staying further proceedings until the original discovery order is obeyed; dismissing all or part of the action; or entering judgment by default against the disobedient party. The court may also hold the disobedient party in contempt or require the party failing to obey the order (or its attorney, or both) to pay the opponent's reasonable expenses, including attorney's fees, caused by the failure.

Lost in the detail of FRCP 37(b) is the crucial point—do not disobey a federal discovery order. It permits your adversary to gain a huge advantage in the battle for credibility with the court, which is a giant step on the road to winning the lawsuit. This may be a more severe punishment to your client than any remedy issued under FRCP 37, and a stain on your reputation in the court in which you will continue to practice long after the case is over.

FRCP 37(c) applies these same general remedies for a party's failures in connection with its initial discovery obligations under FRCP 26, and to its responses to requests for admissions under FRCP 36. A party who fails to disclose information required by FRCP 26(a) and (e) faces the automatic sanction of prohibition of use of the information as evidence in the case, and, upon motion, economic sanctions and/or the other FRCP 37 remedies. The court may also inform the jury of the party's failure to make the disclosure. Where a party fails to admit the genuineness of any document or the truth of any matter in a request for admissions under FRCP 36, the other party may seek an order requiring payment of its reasonable expenses, including attorneys fees, incurred in making the proof of the matter at issue. The court shall award the sanctions unless the party failing to admit had good reason to do so.

FRCP 37(d), oddly out of sequence, provides remedies for the specific discovery misconduct by a party such as failure to appear for a deposition, provide answers to interrogatories, or respond to a document request. Though FRCP 37(d) authorizes the court to award some, but not all, of the FRCP 37(b)(2) remedies in the event of these misdeeds, the case law has permitted the courts

RULE 37. FAILURE TO MAKE DISCLOSURE OR COOPERATE IN DISCOVERY; SANCTIONS

flexibility to choose the remedies to be applied. The Rule is clear that a party may not decline to respond to these discovery devices because it believes that they are objectionable; it is the objecting party's responsibility to move for a protective order rather than sit silently.

A litigator with an objection to a pending discovery request must carefully review the applicable federal rule to determine whether he must make a motion for a protective order, or may informally assert his objection and wait for his adversary to seek the court's assistance. In most situations it is a bad idea to ignore a discovery request in a federal action and wait for the seeking party to take action. Local rules may permit counsel to notify the court of a discovery problem by letter rather than formal motion. Never take to the court a discovery dispute that you have not made a serious effort to resolve in discussions with your adversary.

FRCP 37(g) authorizes the court to award economic sanctions, including attorney's fees, where a party (or its attorney) has failed to participate in good faith in the development and submission of a proposed discovery plan, as required by FRCP 26(f).

FRCP 37 is long and difficult to follow, and has been amended so that it says a little bit about many different discovery situations. One of the less obvious messages, however, is that in addition to enforcing discovery requests, there is a clear message that federal courts are increasingly impatient with attempts by attorneys to gain advantage through overly aggressive discovery tactics. A thoughtful litigator will keep this in mind throughout all discovery activities.

Rule 45. Subpoena

(a) Form; Issuance.

(1) Every subpoena shall

(A) state the name of the court from which it is issued; and

(B) state the title of the action, the name of the court in which it is pending, and its civil action number; and

(C) command each person to whom it is directed to attend and give testimony or to produce and permit inspection and copying of designated books, documents or tangible things in the possession, custody or control of that person, or to permit inspection of premises, at a time and place therein specified; and

(D) set forth the text of subdivisions (c) and (d) of this rule.

A command to produce evidence or to permit inspection may be joined with a command to appear at trial or hearing or at deposition, or may be issued separately.

(2) A subpoena commanding attendance at a trial or hearing shall issue from the court for the district in which the hearing or trial is to be held. A subpoena for attendance at a deposition shall issue from the court for the district designated by the notice of deposition as the district in which the deposition is to be taken. If separate from a subpoena commanding the attendance of a person, a subpoena for production or inspection shall issue from the court for the district in which the production or inspection is to be made.

(3) The clerk shall issue a subpoena, signed but otherwise in blank, to a party requesting it, who shall complete it before service. An attorney as officer of the court may also issue and sign a subpoena on behalf of

(A) a court in which the attorney is authorized to practice; or

(**B**) a court for a district in which a deposition or production is compelled by the subpoena, if the deposition or production pertains to an action pending in a court in which the attorney is authorized to practice.

(b) Service.

(**1**) A subpoena may be served by any person who is not a party and is not less than 18 years of age. Service of a subpoena upon a person named therein shall be made by delivering a copy thereof to such person and, if the person's attendance is commanded, by tendering to that person the fees for one day's attendance and the mileage allowed by law. When the subpoena is issued on behalf of the United States or an officer or agency thereof, fees and mileage need not be tendered. Prior notice of any commanded production of documents and things or inspection of premises before trial shall be served on each party in the manner prescribed by Rule 5(b).

(**2**) Subject to the provisions of clause (ii) of subparagraph (c)(3)(A) of this rule, a subpoena may be served at any place within the district of the court by which it is issued, or at any place without the district that is within 100 miles of the place of the deposition, hearing, trial, production, or inspection specified in the subpoena or at any place within the state where a state statute or rule of court permits service of a subpoena issued by a state court of general jurisdiction sitting in the place of the deposition, hearing, trial, production, or inspection specified in the subpoena. When a statute of the United States provides therefor, the court upon proper application and cause shown may authorize the service of a subpoena at any other place. A subpoena directed to a witness in a foreign country who is a national or resident of the United States shall issue under the circumstances and in the manner and be served as provided in Title 28, U.S.C. § 1783.

(**3**) Proof of service when necessary shall be made by filing with the clerk of the court by which the subpoena is issued a statement of the date and manner of service and of the names of the persons served, certified by the person who made the service.

(c) Protection of Persons Subject to Subpoenas.

(1) A party or an attorney responsible for the issuance and service of a subpoena shall take reasonable steps to avoid imposing undue burden or expense on a person subject to that subpoena. The court on behalf of which the subpoena was issued shall enforce this duty and impose upon the party or attorney in breach of this duty an appropriate sanction, which may include, but is not limited to, lost earnings and a reasonable attorney's fee.

(2) (A) A person commanded to produce and permit inspection and copying of designated books, papers, documents or tangible things, or inspection of premises need not appear in person at the place of production or inspection unless commanded to appear for deposition, hearing or trial.

(B) Subject to paragraph (d)(2) of this rule, a person commanded to produce and permit inspection and copying may, within 14 days after service of the subpoena or before the time specified for compliance if such time is less than 14 days after service, serve upon the party or attorney designated in the subpoena written objection to inspection or copying of any or all of the designated materials or of the premises. If objection is made, the party serving the subpoena shall not be entitled to inspect and copy the materials or inspect the premises except pursuant to an order of the court by which the subpoena was issued. If objection has been made, the party serving the subpoena may, upon notice to the person commanded to produce, move at any time for an order to compel the production. Such an order to compel production shall protect any person who is not a party or an officer of a party from significant expense resulting from the inspection and copying commanded.

(3) (A) On timely motion, the court by which a subpoena was issued shall quash or modify the subpoena if it

(i) fails to allow reasonable time for compliance;

(ii) requires a person who is not a party or an officer of a party to travel to a place more than 100 miles from the place where that person resides, is employed or regularly transacts business in person, except that, subject to the provisions of clause (c)(3)(B)(iii) of this rule, such a person may in order to attend trial be commanded to travel from any such place within the state in which the trial is held, or

(iii) requires disclosure of privileged or other protected matter and no exception or waiver applies, or

(iv) subjects a person to undue burden.

(B) If a subpoena

(i) requires disclosure of a trade secret or other confidential research, development, or commercial information, or

(ii) requires disclosure of an unretained expert's opinion or information not describing specific events or occurrences in dispute and resulting from the expert's study made not at the request of any party, or

(iii) requires a person who is not a party or an officer of a party to incur substantial expense to travel more than 100 miles to attend trial, the court may, to protect a person subject to or affected by the subpoena, quash or modify the subpoena or, if the party in whose behalf the subpoena is issued shows a substantial need for the testimony or material that cannot be otherwise met without undue hardship and assures that the person to whom the subpoena is addressed will be reasonably compensated, the court may order appearance or production only upon specified conditions.

(d) Duties in Responding to Subpoena.

(1) A person responding to a subpoena to produce documents shall produce them as they are kept in the usual course of business or shall organize and label them to correspond with the categories in the demand.

(2) When information subject to a subpoena is withheld on a claim that it is privileged or subject to protection as trial preparation materials, the claim shall be made expressly and shall be supported by a description of the nature of the documents, communications, or things not produced that is sufficient to enable the demanding party to contest the claim.

(e) Contempt. Failure by any person without adequate excuse to obey a subpoena served upon that person may be deemed a contempt of the court from which the subpoena issued. An adequate cause for failure to obey exists when a subpoena purports to require a non-party to attend or produce at a place not within the limits provided by clause (ii) of subparagraph (c)(3)(A).

Commentary

By Janis M. Meyer
Dewey Ballantine LLP

Introduction

Rule 45 sets forth the procedures for obtaining discovery from persons not a party to litigation. While a subpoena is not required to obtain discovery from a party to the litigation, a subpoena must be used to compel testimony, production, inspection, and copying of documents or tangible things, and inspection of premises from a person or entity not a party to the litigation. See Rules 30(b)(1), 34(c). Rule 45 also applies to subpoenas for the attendance of witnesses and production of documents in arbitrations under the Alternative Dispute Resolution Act. 28 USCS § 656. FRCP 45 should be read in conjunction with the other rules applicable to discovery.

Although nonparty testimony or inspection and copying of documents and things may be obtained voluntarily, service of a subpoena is the better practice, particularly where testimony is sought. A nonparty who has not been subpoenaed has no obligation to appear. In addition, if a party expecting a voluntary appearance has not served a subpoena and the witness does not appear at the scheduled time, that party may be ordered to pay the expenses of the other parties who appeared for the deposition, including their reasonable attorney's fees. See Rule 30(g)(2).

Rule 45 was revised extensively in 1991. The 1991 amendments were intended to clarify and enlarge the protections for subpoenaed witnesses. These amendments also facilitate discovery of documents and other information from nonparties without the need for a deposition, make service of subpoenas in districts other than where the case is pending easier, and authorize compulsion of witnesses for trial within the state in which the court sits even if they are not within the district issuing the subpoena. See notes of Advisory Committee on 1991 amendments. Although many of the principles embodied in Rule 45 prior to the 1991 amendments remain, pre-amendment case law should be examined in conjunction with the amendments to ensure that the section of the Rule cited has not been altered either by the amendments themselves or the post-1991 case law interpreting them.

Form and Issuance of Subpoena

Rule 45(a) describes the requirements relating to the form and issuance of the subpoena. Because a subpoena is a court order and is used to command a witness (either a person or an entity) not otherwise before the court to perform certain acts, there is in general strict adherence to these formal requirements. A subpoena must state the name of the court from which it is issued, the title of the action, the name of the court in which the action is pending, and its civil action number, and contain a command to the subpoenaed witness to attend and give testimony or produce the items designated therein at a specified time and place. The subpoena must also contain the text of Rules 45(c) and (d) which, as discussed below, describe the protections available to witnesses subject to subpoenas as well as their duties in responding. In practice, this requirement can be satisfied by attaching a copy of these sections to the subpoena.

Scope of Subpoena

The scope of discovery available through a subpoena is the same as that available under Rule 34 and the other discovery rules. (See notes of Advisory Committee Note on 1970 amendments. Interrogatories are not available, however.) Thus, a corporation, partnership, association or governmental agency may be named as the deponent and be required to designate a witness or witnesses to testify on its behalf. Rule 30(b)(6). A subpoenaed person or entity may be required to produce documents or tangible things in its possession, custody, or control, and to permit inspection of premises. Rule 45(a)(1)(C). Production is not limited to documents or information located within the district from which the subpoena was issued but is limited to documents in the subpoenaed witness's possession or in witness's custody or control wherever the documents are located. As is the case under Rule 34, the documents sought need not be in hard copy but may be in electronic format. See Rule 34(a).

Prior to the 1991 amendments, a subpoena for the production of documents or things (subpoena duces tecum) could be served only in conjunction with a trial or deposition subpoena for trial or deposition testimony (subpoena ad testificandum). After the 1991 amendments, Rule 45(a)(1) makes it clear that a subpoena duces tecum and a subpoena for testimony may be served together or separately. Rule 45(c)(2)(A) reinforces this by stating that a subpoena for inspection and copying of books or tangible things does not require a personal appearance unless there is also a notice for deposition or for hearing or trial testimony.

A subpoena that seeks production of documents may include the document request on the face of the subpoena or attach the document request as an appendix to the subpoena. The document request may include definitions and instructions similar to those included in a Rule 34 request.

The issue of how broad the document request can or should be depends on a number of factors. One is the nature of the case. For example, a fifteen-page document request seeking all documents the third-party has relating to the defendant's activities may be deemed burdensome in a small personal injury matter but quite reasonable in an antitrust matter.

In addition, the serving party should balance the need for the documents sought against the potential expense and burden of motion practice. A court may consider a very broad document request more burdensome when the discovery is sought from a nonparty rather than from a party. (A litigant should nevertheless resist any temptation to name a nonparty as a defendant solely for the purpose of making discovery easier. Such a step would be an obvious invitation for sanctions.)

Timing is another factor to be considered. Serving a broad document request at an early stage in the litigation may succeed even if there is a dispute over production. Serving the same request with a discovery deadline looming may result in last-minute motion practice and no document production. A narrowly focused request is less likely to meet the same fate.

The scope of documents sought will necessarily have to be determined on a case-by-case basis. In any case, it should be remembered that opposing a motion to quash or for a protective order can be expensive and time-consuming and divert attention from the issues in the litigation itself.

Whether documents are in a witness's possession, custody, or control is a question of fact that has arisen frequently in the context of Rule 45 as well as under Rule 34. However, although there is no explicit indication in either Rule 34 or Rule 45, as a practical matter the balancing that is inherent in any consideration of discovery disputes may result in different conclusions depending upon the status of the person or entity from whom the documents are sought. A court may weigh the nonparty status of the subpoenaed witness together with the burdensomeness of producing from distant locations and conclude that production that may have been reasonable from a party should not be compelled from a nonparty even if the documents are within the nonparty's control. This analysis is fact-specific, and whether documents, even if deemed to be in a witness's possession, custody, or control, must be produced in response to a subpoena will ultimately depend on the circumstances of the case.

Location and Method of Issuance of Subpoena

Rule 45(a)(2) provides that a subpoena for:

> attendance at a trial or a hearing must issue from the court for the district in which the hearing or trial is to be held;

> a deposition must issue from the court for the district in which the deposition is noticed to be taken;

production or inspection must issue from the court for the district in which the production or inspection is to be made.

The choice of the issuing court may have strategic consequences in the event there is a dispute over the enforceability of the subpoena: a motion to quash or to compel must be made to the court in the district from which the subpoena was issued. Rule 45(c)(3)(A). Although there are territorial limits on a subpoena's reach, there are situations (e.g., where judicial districts do not cover large geographic regions) where a subpoena can be issued in alternative jurisdictions and reach the person from whom discovery is sought. If there is a choice, a party contemplating serving a subpoena may wish to examine the nuances of a district's rulings on motions to quash or compel before issuing a subpoena.

Prior to the 1991 amendments, the clerk of the issuing court had to issue a subpoena; now, however, an attorney may issue and sign a subpoena for a district court in which he is authorized to practice (Rule 45(a)(3)(A)), or for a court in the district in which the deposition is to be taken or production is to be made if the discovery "pertains to an action pending in a court in which the attorney is authorized to practice" (Rule 45(a)(3)(B)). This means that an attorney can issue and sign a subpoena in any district in the United States in which discovery is sought provided that he is admitted (even only pro hac vice) in the district in which the action is pending.

Service of Subpoena

Rule 45(b) sets forth the requirements for service of a subpoena. If the subpoena is for attendance at a deposition or trial, witness fees must be tendered for one day's attendance and the mileage allowed by law as set forth in 28 USCS § 1821. A subpoena may be served "by any person who is not a party and is not less than 18 years of age." Rule 45(b)(1). As in the case of the requirements for issuing a subpoena, failing to comply with these formal requirements may result in the subpoena being quashed on technical grounds.

Method of Service

Rule 45(b)(1) requires that service be made by "delivering a copy" of the subpoena to the person or entity summoned. This language has been held to require personal service and not to allow for the alternative or substituted methods of service permitted under Rule 4. However, although this remains the majority view, a few recent cases have permitted alternative methods of service, particularly where the traditional method of personal service could not be accomplished despite diligent efforts by the serving party. See, e.g., *Cordius Trust v. Kummerfeld*, 45 Fed. R. Serv. 3d 1151 (S.D. N.Y. 2000); *King v. Crown Plastering Corp.*, 170 F.R.D. 355 (E.D. N.Y. 1997); *Doe v. Hersemann*, 155 F.R.D. 630 (N.D. Ind. 1994).

A party serving a subpoena for production of documents and things or inspection of premises before trial must serve prior notice on each party to the litigation. Rule 45(b)(1). "Prior" means prior to service of the subpoena, not prior to the production or inspection. This permits the other parties to the litigation to object to the production or take other appropriate action. Prior notice of a deposition is also required. (See Rule 30(b)(1) requiring reasonable notice to every other party to the action.)

Rule 45(b)(3) requires that proof of service "when necessary" be filed with the clerk. Prior to the 1991 amendments, proof of service was required for the clerk to issue the subpoena. Now such filing is optional and need only be made if a dispute arises over service.

Location of Service

Rule 45(b)(2) describes where a subpoena may be served. It should be read in conjunction with Rule 45(c)(3)(A)(ii) as well as Rule 45(c)(3)(B)(iii). Rule 45(b)(2) provides that a subpoena may be served:

within the district of the court issuing the subpoena;

outside the district if within 100 miles of the place where the deposition, hearing, trial or production is to be held; or any place within the state if a state statute or rule of court would permit service of a subpoena issued by a state court sitting where the testimony or production is to occur.

Subparagraph (b)(2) is subject to Rule 45(c)(3)(A)(ii) which provides that:

> the issuing court "shall" quash or modify a subpoena "if it requires a person who is not a party or an officer of a party to travel to a place more than 100 miles from the place where that person resides, is employed, or regularly transacts business in person", but

> any person may be ordered to travel from any place within a state to attend trial, subject to Rule 45(c)(3)(B)(iii).

Rule 45(c)(3)(B)(iii) provides that a subpoena requiring a person who is not a party or an officer of a party to incur substantial expense to travel more than 100 miles to attend trial may be quashed or modified; or the court may, upon a showing of substantial need, order appearance or production only upon specified conditions.

In practice, these provisions mean that the serving party:

> must ascertain where the person from whom discovery is sought lives, works, or regularly transacts business in person and designate the place for testimony or production within 100 miles of one of those locations;

> must issue the subpoena from a court in the district in which the place designated for testimony or production is located; and

> must serve the subpoena within the district in which the issuing court is located or, if not within the district, within 100 miles of where the discovery is to occur; or

> may, if it would be permitted by statute or court rule of a state sitting where the discovery is to occur, serve anywhere within the state.

Thus, for example, if a witness lives, works, or regularly transacts business within 100 miles of New York County, which is located in the Southern District of New York, New York County can be designated as the place for testimony or production and the subpoena should be issued from a court in the Southern District. The subpoena must then be served on the witness in the Southern District or within 100 miles of New York County, where the discovery is to occur. This means that the witness may be served in parts of Connecticut and New Jersey (and any other state within 100 miles of the place where the discovery is to occur) as well as in New York State.

Further, state law in New York permits service of a subpoena issued by a state court (with some exceptions for lower courts) to be served anywhere in the state. Accordingly, if the witness is within New York State, he can be served anywhere in the state whether or not it is 100 miles from New York County. Nevertheless, this is subject to the provision that if the witness is not a party or an officer of a party and chooses to challenge the subpoena, any subpoena other than a trial subpoena shall be quashed or modified if it requires a witness to travel more than 100 miles from where he resides, is employed or regularly transacts business. Rule 45(c)(3)(A)(ii). In addition, a subpoena requiring a witness to travel more than 100 miles to testify at trial may be quashed or modified unless the serving party shows substantial need. Rule 45(c)(3)(B)(iii). Thus, the witness may be served in Buffalo, New York, which is more than 100 miles from New York County. However, if the witness resides, is employed and regularly transacts business in Buffalo or some other location more than 100 miles from New York County, he may successfully move to quash or modify the subpoena depending upon the type of subpoena served.

A litigant should consider the ability to serve subpoenas outside the state in choosing a forum. New York, for example, does not permit service of a state court subpoena outside the state. Thus, it is not possible to compel an out-of-state witness's trial testimony in state court, even if he is located only five miles across the Hudson River in New Jersey. The party seeking the testimony has to rely on deposition testimony if he cannot persuade the witness to appear. The same witness could be compelled to testify at trial in federal court because he is located within 100 miles of the courthouse. Thus, a thoughtful plaintiff (and a defendant considering removal) should consider the state court rules relating to subpoenas when making a choice as to whether to proceed in state or federal court.

Rule 45(b)(2) also provides that, where a federal statute provides for service of a subpoena, the court may authorize service at any place provided in that statute. Further, a U.S. national or resident who is in a foreign country shall be served in the manner provided in 28 USCS § 1783.

If discovery is sought from a nonparty non-U.S. person or entity that cannot be served in the U.S., a Rule 45 subpoena cannot be used because the U.S. court has no power to compel discovery from a person or entity not subject to its jurisdiction. Accordingly, the party seeking discovery must use some form of international legal assistance to obtain the discovery sought. The United States is a party to the Hague Convention of 18 March 1970 on the Taking of Evidence Abroad in Civil or Commercial Matters and the Inter-American Convention on Letters Rogatory, each of which provides methods and procedures for obtaining evidence in signatory countries. See 28 USCS § 1781.

Protections for Subpoenaed Persons

Rule 45(c) sets forth the protections for subpoenaed persons. The section sets out the territorial limitations described above and describes the procedural mechanisms available to the serving party as well as the subpoenaed witness to compel or prevent discovery.

Rule 45(c)(1) requires that the party or attorney issuing and serving the subpoena avoid imposing undue burden or expense on the subpoenaed person and provides for sanctions for breach of this duty. This provision is particularly significant given that attorneys, as a result of the 1991 amendments, are free to sign and issue subpoenas themselves. A sanction may include, but is not limited to, reimbursement of lost earnings and reasonable attorney's fees.

Objections

Rule 45(c)(2)(B) permits a witness served with a subpoena duces tecum to serve written objections to inspection or copying of all or part of the designated materials or of the premises within 14 days after service of the subpoena or before the time specified for compliance if it is less than 14 days after service. If such an objection is made, the subpoenaed person or entity need not produce the requested materials unless ordered to do so by the court that issued the subpoena. Objections may be made only with respect to inspection and copying. Opposition to a subpoena for testimony must take the form of a motion to quash or a motion for a protective order.

The right to object is provided for "a person commanded to produce and permit copying and inspection" (Rule 45(c)(2)(B)), and there is no explicit provision for a party to the litigation to object or otherwise move with respect to a subpoena. However, if a litigating party's own rights (and not merely its strategic position in the lawsuit) are implicated by the subpoena, it has the right to object or make an appropriate motion. For example, if a subpoena to a nonparty could result in production of a party's privileged or otherwise protected documents, the party may have no choice but to move to quash or for a protective order preventing or limiting production in order to avoid a waiver.

Motions to Compel or Quash

A motion to compel must be made in the issuing court. Rule 45(c)(2)(B). A motion to quash is also made in the issuing court. Rule 45(c)(3)(A). As noted above, this is a factor to consider in determining in which district to issue the subpoena. However, a motion for a protective order should be made in the court in which the action is pending (Rule 26(c)) or, in the case of a deposition, in the court where the action is pending or in the district where the deposition is being taken. Rules 26(c), 30(d)(3). Thus, the rules should be reviewed carefully before a motion is made to ensure that it is in the proper court.

Rule 45(c)(3) contains the requirements for quashing or modifying a subpoena. Subparagraph (c)(3)(A) describes the circumstances in which a court shall quash or modify a subpoena. Subparagraph (c)(3)(B) describes circumstances in which the court may quash or modify a subpoena or, upon a showing of substantial need by the serving party, order compliance upon specified conditions.

A subpoena shall be quashed or modified if:

it does not allow reasonable time for compliance. Rule 45(c)(3)(A)(i). A reasonable time may vary from case to case. Providing 14 days for a nonparty to produce a large volume of documents may be unreasonable whereas providing three days for a nonparty to testify in a case where a preliminary injunction hearing is about to be held may be reasonable. In practice, many attorneys give the same notice periods provided for parties in Rules 30 and 34.

as discussed above, it requires a person who is not a party or an officer of a party to travel more than 100 miles from where he lives, works or regularly transacts business. Rule 45(c)(3)(A)(ii).

it requires disclosure of privileged or other protected matter. Rule 45(c)(3)(A)(iii).

it subjects a person to undue burden. Rule 45(c)(3)(A)(iv). This provision covers a variety of situations not specifically listed in subparagraphs (c)(3)(A) or (B). Thus, where a document request is too broad or the subpoena seeks documents from far-flung locations, a motion will fall under this provision. A subpoenaed witness's nonparty status may render burdensome discovery that would be proper when sought from a party. What constitutes an undue burden is case-specific and will vary depending upon the circumstances.

A subpoena may be quashed or modified if:

it seeks disclosure of a trade secret or other confidential research, development or commercial information. Rule 45(c)(3)(B)(i);

it requires an unretained expert to disclose an opinion or information that was not developed at the request of a party. Rule 45(c)(3)(B)(ii); or

as discussed above, it requires a person who is not a party or an officer of a party to incur substantial expense to travel more than 100 miles to attend trial. Rule 45(c)(3)(B)(iii).

Nevertheless, the court may order appearance or production upon "specified conditions" if the party seeking the testimony or production shows a substantial need that cannot otherwise be met without undue hardship and assures that the witness will be reasonably compensated. Rule 45(c)(3)(B). The showing of substantial need is similar to that required to overcome work product protection. See Rule 26(b)(3).

Reimbursement for Costs

If the court orders production, any person who is not a party or an officer of a party shall be protected from significant expense resulting from such inspection and copying. Rule 45(c)(2)(B). A court may fix expenses prior to production or may make that determination after the production is completed. See Advisory Committee Notes, 1991 amendments. Nevertheless, a subpoenaed person or entity is wise to raise the issue of reimbursement for costs prior to production either by objection or motion to ensure that failure to do so will not be deemed a waiver.

Costs reimbursable under Rule 45(c)(2)(B) may be broader than those awarded to a prevailing party under 28 USCS § 1920, and the court may award legal fees. For example, a court recently awarded a subpoenaed entity a portion of the legal fees it incurred in seeking permission to produce documents from a court in the non-U.S. jurisdiction where the documents were located. *First American Corporation v. Price Waterhouse LLP*, 184 F.R.D. 234 (S.D. N.Y. 1998).

Responsibilities of a Subpoenaed Person

Rule 45(d) sets forth the subpoenaed witness's duties in responding to a subpoena. Rule 45(d)(1) mirrors the requirement of Rule 34(b) that documents be produced as they are kept in the ordinary course of business or labeled to correspond to the categories of documents sought in the document request.

Claims of Privilege

Rule 45(d)(2) creates an obligation that may have an impact on the content of a subpoenaed witness's objections. Where a claim of privilege is asserted, it must be made "expressly" and must include a description of the privileged material sufficient to enable the serving party to contest the privilege claim. This raises the issue of when such a description must be provided. A general objection on the grounds of privilege, work product, or other applicable protection should be made at the time objections to the subpoena are made to avoid any risk that the objection may be waived. This requirement places little burden on the subpoenaed witness. However, in practice, it may be difficult to identify which documents will actually be withheld on privilege grounds when objections are made, particularly where the subpoenaed person or entity hopes to be able to narrow the scope of production or to determine what is actually being sought before beginning a search for documents. The most practical approach, and one that is commonly followed, is to preserve the privilege objection by including it in general objections to a subpoena and to require a privilege log only after document production has occurred. Any other requirement places a greater burden on nonparties than on parties who in practice supply privilege logs after they have produced documents.

Resolution of Disputes

Rule 45 does not contain on its face any "meet and confer" requirement before a motion to quash or compel is made although local court rules may impose such a requirement. For example see Local Civil Rules for the Southern and Eastern Districts of New York, Rule 37.3(a) (applicable to Eastern District only). Thus, in the absence of a local rule, the serving party or the subpoenaed person or entity is free to move to compel or to quash without attempting to resolve or narrow the dispute. However, the question requires further consideration. A party or person seeking a protective order is required to make a good faith effort to resolve the dispute prior to making a motion. Rule 26(c). Because a motion to quash may be accompanied by a motion for a protective order, or a motion to compel may result in a cross-motion for a protective order, it would appear to be a better practice to try to resolve the issues in dispute before resorting to motion practice, regardless of the type of motion. A discussion between counsel may result in a narrowing of the subpoena or, at the least, an understanding of the other side's position. It may also reduce the likelihood that a court will be annoyed that there was not an attempt to resolve the issues prior to motion practice.

Consequences of Failure to Comply

Rule 45(e) provides that failure to obey a subpoena without adequate excuse may be deemed a contempt of court. The Rule also states that there is an adequate cause for failure to obey when a subpoena requires attendance or production outside the limits of Rule 45(c)(3)(A)(ii), that is, more than 100 miles from the witness's residence, place of employment, or place where he regularly transacts business. However, a subpoenaed witness should consider carefully whether to ignore a subpoena on this ground or any other ground it considers "an adequate excuse." In the event a motion to compel is made, a court may perceive a witness who takes no action in response to a valid subpoena as having disregarded a court order, a result a witness in most circumstances will wish to avoid.

28 U.S.C.S. § 1781 — Transmittal of letter rogatory or request

(a) The Department of State has power, directly, or through suitable channels—

(1) to receive a letter rogatory issued, or request made, by a foreign or international tribunal, to transmit it to the tribunal, officer, or agency in the United States to whom it is addressed, and to receive and return it after execution; and

(2) to receive a letter rogatory issued, or request made, by a tribunal in the United States, to transmit it to the foreign or international tribunal, officer, or agency to whom it is addressed, and to receive and return it after execution.

(b) This section does not preclude—

(1) the transmittal of a letter rogatory or request directly from a foreign or international tribunal to the tribunal, officer, or agency in the United States to whom it is addressed and its return in the same manner; or

(2) the transmittal of a letter rogatory or request directly from a tribunal in the United States to the foreign or international tribunal, officer, or agency to whom it is addressed and its return in the same manner.

Commentary

Janis M. Meyer
Dewey Ballantine LLP

Section 1781 of Title 28, USCS, authorizes the receipt and transmittal of letters rogatory (also known as letters of request) to and from foreign countries and tribunals either through the U.S. Department of State or directly to and from foreign tribunals.

A letter rogatory is a formal request from a court in one country to the competent authority in another country asking that authority to serve process on an individual or entity located there or to order the testimony of a witness or the production of documents or other evidence. Increased international commerce, the proliferation of multi-national corporations, and the associated increase in litigation requiring cross-border service of process or evidence-gathering necessitated the development and improvement of devices to facilitate such litigation.

The enactment and subsequent revision of § 1781 attempted to achieve those goals by providing clear authorization for both the transmission and receipt of letters rogatory for, inter alia, obtaining evidence and testimony abroad for use in proceedings in the United States. S. Rep. No. 88-1580 (1964), reprinted in 1964 U.S.C.C.A.N. 3782, 3782.

Section 1781 authorizes the Department of State to transmit and receive letters rogatory for both evidence and service of process. The statute makes clear, however, that a court may transmit or receive a letter rogatory directly to or from a foreign tribunal without the involvement of the State Department if such a procedure is acceptable in the requested country.

Litigants occasionally find the use of letters rogatory daunting, however, because of the time involved (sometimes six months or a year depending upon the jurisdiction) and the fact that execution of the letter rogatory is purely within the discretion of the foreign state. The need for more certain, timely, and simplified international legal assistance methods has led the United States to enter into several treaties providing for streamlined procedures and requiring the signatories to execute a properly transmitted request. These treaties include the Convention on the Service Abroad of Judicial and Extra-Judicial Documents in Civil or Commercial Matters, 20 U.S.T. 361, 1969 U.S.T. LEXIS 152 (Hague Service Convention); the Hague Convention on the Taking of Evidence Abroad in Civil or Commercial Matters, 23 U.S.T. 2555, 1970 U.S.T. Lexis 497 (Hague Evidence Convention); and the Inter-American Convention on Letters Rogatory and Additional Protocol, 1975 U.S.T. LEXIS 589 (Inter-American Service Convention).

Letters Rogatory in General

Procedures for drafting a letter rogatory for service or for the taking of evidence and transmitting it to the requested country vary depending upon the rules of the foreign jurisdiction. For example, some jurisdictions will accept a request directly from the U.S. court to their own court, a procedure authorized by § 1781(b)(2). Thus, a litigant can submit the letter rogatory to the U.S. court and have the court issue and transmit the letter to the court in the requested country for execution. This procedure can result in expeditious treatment of the request.

Other jurisdictions require a much more formal procedure, involving submission to the U.S. court, followed by transmission to the State Department for transmission to the diplomatic authority in the foreign jurisdiction, which will then determine whether to forward the request to the appropriate court. There is no certainty that the letter will be executed by the foreign authority because execution of a letter rogatory without an applicable treaty is discretionary. In each case, the process is initiated by motion to the court in which the case is pending, under § 1781(a)(2) or (b)(2) depending upon the procedure requested.

A litigant should retain counsel in the jurisdiction in which assistance is sought as early as possible in the proceedings to determine the procedures that jurisdiction prefers and ensure that the letters rogatory or letters of request are drafted properly.

Letters Rogatory for Service

If the party to be served is located in a country that is a signatory to the Hague Service Convention, the Convention's procedures must be utilized. *Volkswagenwerk Aktiengesellschaft v. Schlunk*, 486 U.S. 694, 100 L. Ed. 2d 722, 108 S. Ct. 2104 (1988). The Hague Service Convention greatly simplifies the procedures for use of a letter rogatory (called a request in the Convention) seeking service abroad. The Hague Service Convention provides for transmission of the documents to be served through a Central Authority, or, if authorized by the country in which service is to be made, directly from the U.S. court to the party to be served. Depending upon the foreign jurisdiction, the Hague Service Convention significantly shortens the time required to complete service. (The reference to "Hague Convention" is imprecise and applies to a large number of conventions dealing with different countries and a range of subjects. See *http://www.hcch.net/index.html*, and the History and the Notes following USCS FRCP 4.)

The Inter-American Service Convention provides a mechanism for service of documents in signatory countries through Central Authorities. The Inter-American Service Convention authorizes the use of letters rogatory for the performance of procedural acts of a formal nature (e.g., service of process, summonses, or subpoenas). Although use of the Inter-American Service Convention is not mandatory under U.S. law, the procedures ensure that a defendant cannot claim later that it was not served properly. The Inter-American Service Convention, although requiring more formal procedures than the Hague Service Convention, ensures that if the proper procedures are followed, the letter rogatory will be executed.

Both the Hague Service Convention and the Inter-American Service Convention set forth the proper procedures to follow, e.g., translation of documents, the necessary certifications and the appropriate governmental entities to transmit or receive documents.

If there is no such treaty, use of a letter rogatory transmitted through the Department of State to the competent authority in the foreign state may be the only method of effective service. Making direct service in a foreign country without using an applicable treaty or letters rogatory through diplomatic channels may violate that country's laws. Even if a U.S. court were to find service effective, in all likelihood the foreign state will refuse to enforce any judgment obtained in the proceeding. Thus, if the defendant does not have assets in the U.S. against which the judgment can be enforced, a wiser course is to effect service by letter rogatory either pursuant to the appropriate convention or through diplomatic channels.

The Taking of Evidence Abroad

Letters rogatory also provide the means for obtaining evidence from abroad. U.S. litigants often perceive letters rogatory to be a burdensome method of discovery, even when they can utilize the procedures of the Hague Evidence Convention, which greatly simplifies the letters rogatory process. This perception is due in part to the fact that few, if any, foreign jurisdictions permit the broad range of pre-trial evidence-gathering practiced in the U.S. and litigants may believe they will not be able to obtain the evidence they seek through the use of letters rogatory or other means. This belief, although on occasion justified, is more often based on lack of experience with such international procedures or a failure to follow them properly. The fact remains that the use of letters rogatory and to a greater extent the Hague Evidence Convention often provides an efficient means of obtaining evidence abroad.

Neither the use of letters rogatory nor the Hague Evidence Convention is mandatory where the foreign entity or individual is subject to the jurisdiction of a U.S. court. *Societe Nationale Industrielle Aerospatiale v. United States Dist. Court for Southern Dist.*, 482 U.S. 522, 96 L. Ed. 2d 461, 107 S. Ct. 2542 (1987). Nevertheless, there may be cases where evidence is sought from a non-party not subject to jurisdiction in the U.S. In such a case, unless the non-party appears voluntarily, international legal assistance methods provide the only means of obtaining the discovery sought.

Further, even where a party or non-party is subject to U.S. jurisdiction, the evidence sought may be located in a country with laws against production without a formal request from the U.S. court. Courts often use a balancing test to determine whether principles of international comity require the use of international legal assistance measures even though the individual or entity from whom discovery is sought is subject to jurisdiction here. It may be more efficient to avoid motion practice on this issue and use letters rogatory or the Hague Evidence Convention to obtain the testimony or documents.

The Hague Evidence Convention

The Hague Evidence Convention simplifies the procedures for obtaining evidence abroad in a number of respects. A Letter of Request, submitted in conformity with the Convention's procedures, must be honored unless the act requested does not fall within the functions of that country's judiciary; the requested country considers that its sovereignty or security would be prejudiced thereby; or it has made a specific reservation preventing the act requested from being executed.

The Hague Evidence Convention applies only to civil or commercial matters and requires that evidence requested be for use in a judicial proceeding, commenced or contemplated. The Convention authorizes three different methods for obtaining evidence abroad. These include the use of a Letter of Request, the taking of evidence before diplomatic officers and consular agents, and appointment of special commissioners to take evidence.

If a litigant determines to use a Letter of Request, the application is made to the court in which the case is pending. Article 3 specifies the information to be supplied in the Letter of Request and the standard form appended to the Hague Evidence Convention is fairly straightforward. A Letter of Request may seek both documents and testimony. A litigant may also request that certain procedures be followed (e.g., testimony under oath or use of a stenographer to record the testimony Article 9) and that the law of privilege of the Requesting State be applicable as well as that of the state in which the testimony will be given or the documents produced.

An important feature of the Hague Evidence Convention is that the Letter of Request does not need to be sent to the State Department for transmission. The Convention requires that every signatory country designate a Central Authority to receive, process, execute, and return letters of request. The U.S. court (and often, in practice, the litigant seeking the evidence) transmits the letter directly to the Central Authority of the requested state or, if authorized by that country, directly to the court in the foreign jurisdiction having jurisdiction over the individual or entity from whom the evidence is sought. Equally important, the Hague Evidence Convention provides for the use of compulsory measures in the foreign country to obtain the evidence sought (Article 10).

To avoid a foreign jurisdiction's refusal to honor a request for documents on the ground that it seeks pre-trial discovery (Article 23), the documents sought should be identified specifically in the Letter of Request, including the author, recipient, date, subject, and content, as this will increase the chances that a Letter of Request will be granted. Further, the Letter of Request should make it clear that the documents and testimony are being sought for use at trial and not merely to help the requesting party determine whether it has a case.

The Hague Evidence Convention also authorizes taking the testimony of a voluntary witness before a diplomatic officer or consular agent (Articles 15 and 16), or a commissioner (Article 17) in the country in which the evidence is to be taken. Although a Letter of Request may be used in judicial proceedings commenced or contemplated (Article 1), Articles 15 through 17 may only be used if proceedings have already commenced.

Inter-American Service Convention

Although the Inter-American Service Convention provides for the taking of evidence, the U.S. has limited its use to service of documents. Thus, if evidence is sought from a country that is a signatory to the Inter-American Service Convention, traditional letters rogatory must be used.

Regardless of the international legal assistance method contemplated, it is extremely important to retain and consult as early in the proceedings as possible with counsel in the jurisdiction in which the service or evidence-taking is to be effected. Such counsel can advise on local procedures, review the documents to be transmitted and, in many cases, expedite matters when the documents reach the requested jurisdiction. The cost of hiring such counsel will be more than offset by the fact that it will serve to avoid having to redraft letters rogatory or letters of request or having them rejected by the foreign jurisdiction on some technicality.

28 U.S.C.S. § 1782—Assistance to foreign and international tribunals and to litigants before such tribunals

(a) The district court of the district in which a person resides or is found may order him to give his testimony or statement or to produce a document or other thing for use in a proceeding in a foreign or international tribunal, including criminal investigations conducted before formal accusation. The order may be made pursuant to a letter rogatory issued, or request made, by a foreign or international tribunal or upon the application of any interested person and may direct that the testimony or statement be given, or the document or other thing be produced, before a person appointed by the court. By virtue of his appointment, the person appointed has power to administer any necessary oath and take the testimony or statement. The order may prescribe the practice and procedure, which may be in whole or part the practice and procedure of the foreign country or the international tribunal, for taking the testimony or statement or producing the document or other thing. To the extent that the order does not prescribe otherwise, the testimony or statement shall be taken, and the document or other thing produced, in accordance with the Federal Rules of Civil Procedure.

A person may not be compelled to give his testimony or statement or to produce a document or other thing in violation of any legally applicable privilege.

(b) This chapter [28 USCS §§ 1781 et seq.] does not preclude a person within the United States from voluntarily giving his testimony or statement, or producing a document or other thing, for use in a proceeding in a foreign or international tribunal before any person and in any manner acceptable to him.

Commentary

Janis M. Meyer
Dewey Ballantine

The objective of 28 USCS § 1782 is to assist foreign and international litigants in obtaining discovery from individuals or entities located in the United States for use in a foreign proceeding. Subsection (a) vests exclusive subject matter jurisdiction in the district court of the district in which "a person" resides (or is found) to order "him" to give testimony or to produce documentary evidence for use in the foreign tribunal.

Because one of the underlying purposes of § 1782 is to encourage foreign countries to provide similar accommodations to U.S. courts, judicial assistance under the statute is not dependent upon reciprocity. Thus, it is irrelevant whether the foreign jurisdiction in question has a comparable device through which an American tribunal or litigant can obtain foreign discovery. Section 1782 must, however, be read in conjunction with applicable treaties, and will be superseded by a subsequently signed, contradictory agreement.

Application for Judicial Assistance

An application for judicial assistance pursuant to § 1782(a) requires only that: (1) the person from whom discovery is sought reside (or may be found) in the district of the district court to which the application is made; (2) the discovery be for use in a proceeding before a foreign tribunal; and (3) the application be made by a foreign or international tribunal or by any other "interested person." The request may be made through a letter rogatory or similar request issued by a foreign or international tribunal or, as noted, upon application by any interested person. The term "any interested person," as used in subsection (a), has been interpreted broadly to encompass not only parties to the foreign or international litigation, but also various other individuals and entities, including private corporations, investigative bodies, foreign legal affairs ministries, attorneys general and other prosecutors. Notably, the foreign litigant need not seek the requested discovery from the tribunal before which the foreign proceeding is pending prior to making a § 1782 application.

28 U.S.C.S. § 1782—ASSISTANCE TO FOREIGN AND INTERNATIONAL TRIBUNALS AND TO LITIGANTS BEFORE SUCH TRIBUNALS

A principal requirement imposed by § 1782 is that the requested discovery be "for use in a *proceeding* in a foreign or international *tribunal*." The terms "tribunal" and "proceeding" are closely intertwined. A "tribunal," within the meaning of the statute, has been defined broadly to include any official governmental body exercising adjudicatory functions. When § 1782 was amended in 1964, the word "tribunal" was substituted for "court" in order to make clear that assistance under the statute is not confined to proceedings before conventional courts, but is equally available in connection with proceedings before foreign administrative and quasi-judicial agencies. *See* S. Rep. No. 1580, at 3288-89 (1964).

Nonetheless, a governmental body that lacks authority to make a binding adjudication is not a "tribunal" for purposes of § 1782. Thus, a governmental agency whose primary function is to conduct investigations unrelated to judicial or quasi-judicial controversies, or which merely reports its findings to another governmental entity, would not qualify as a "tribunal." An investigating magistrate, by contrast, is a "tribunal" for purposes of § 1782, because its investigative authority is incidental to its adjudicative power. The distinction is one of function, not form or semantics.

A further distinguishing characteristic of a "tribunal" is that the entity does not have an institutional interest in the outcome of the proceeding that would be inconsistent with the concept of impartial adjudication inherent in the term "tribunal." The critical inquiry here is whether there is an absence of any meaningful degree of separation between the prosecutorial and adjudicative functions. Entities presiding over proceedings such as those enforcing tax assessment and currency exchange regulations have been held not to constitute "tribunals" on these grounds.

Although § 1782 applications have been granted in connection with proceedings in various governmental settings, there has been a general reluctance to extend the scope of the statute to proceedings before non-official, non-governmental agencies. Thus, for instance, while governmental or intergovernmental arbitral panels are, like other state-sponsored adjudicatory bodies, considered "tribunals" under § 1782, it has been held, with few exceptions, that private arbitral panels, whose authority arises out of private agreements between parties, are not "tribunals."

Finally, although § 1782 clearly contemplates the existence of a foreign "proceeding," it is not necessary that the proceeding actually be pending at the time the application is made. This was made explicit, at least in the criminal context, in 1996, when § 1782 was amended specifically to include "a criminal investigation conducted *before* a formal accusation" within the definition of a "proceeding in a foreign or international tribunal." Still, whether and to what extent a "proceeding" must be pending, particularly with respect to *non*-criminal matters, is unclear. In fact, courts have divided on this issue, with some requiring that the initiation of proceedings be "imminent," while others look only for reliable indications that proceedings will commence within a reasonable time.

Scope of Assistance

Section 1782(a) provides that discovery may be sought from "a person" who "resides or is found" in the district in which the application for assistance is filed. The target of discovery need not be a party to the litigation, nor is the statute's reach limited to individuals; indeed, the term "person," as used in subsection (a), has been read to encompass various types of organizations, including corporations, partnerships, and other associations. However, sovereign governments, including the United States, do not qualify as "persons" for purposes of this provision, and thus are not proper targets of discovery under the statute. Moreover, although, on its face, § 1782 does not contain an explicit geographical limitation, at least one court has noted that public policy considerations weigh in favor of restricting the scope of the statute to evidence physically located within the United States. *See In re Application of Sarrio, S.A.*, 119 F.3d 143 (2d Cir. 1997).

It should also be stressed that the scope of § 1782 is limited to the court's role in procuring testimony or evidence for use in a foreign tribunal. Thus, requests from foreign tribunals that judgments be enforced, or that property in the United States be sequestered, are beyond the district court's authority under the statute. Moreover, courts have strictly construed § 1782 with respect to the types of discovery available, holding, for instance, that interrogatories and requests for admissions do not constitute "testimony" and are thus not discoverable under the statute.

Discoverability Requirement

Courts are split as to whether § 1782 includes an implicit requirement that the information sought is discoverable in the foreign jurisdiction in which it is to be used. Although a majority of courts have held that § 1782 does not require that the evidence sought be discoverable under foreign law (irrespective of the identity of the requesting party), a number of courts have imposed a so-called "discoverability" requirement, at least in instances where the request is made by a private litigant, as opposed to the foreign tribunal itself.

Under this approach, when the request is made by the foreign tribunal itself, courts presume that the requesting authority has considered and applied its own discovery rules and procedures. Where, however, a private litigant seeks discovery pursuant to § 1782 directly, a number of courts have held that the material sought must be discoverable in the foreign jurisdiction in which it is to be used. This requirement is intended not only to ensure that § 1782 is not used to circumvent the discovery rules of the foreign jurisdiction, but also to ensure that U.S. litigants who find themselves before a foreign tribunal and are thus limited to the discovery procedures of that jurisdiction, are not disadvantaged *vis-à-vis* their foreign adversaries.

Claims of Privilege

The last sentence of § 1782(a) contains an important caveat: "A person may not be compelled to give his testimony or statement or to produce a document or other thing in violation of any legally applicable privilege." Courts have interpreted this provision as recognizing both federal and constitutional privileges, as well as statutory immunity and privileges recognized under foreign law. In determining whether a claim of privilege or statutory immunity should be sustained under § 1782, courts are given wide discretion in balancing the purported interest in preserving the privilege against the applicant's showing of need or hardship.

District Court's Discretion

Judicial assistance under § 1782 is not mandatory. On the contrary, § 1782 gives district courts wide discretion in determining whether, and to what extent, to grant or deny applications for discovery and in tailoring such discovery to avoid attendant problems. A district court may, for example, impose terms or conditions on the discovery, such as to require that a person compelled to testify be reasonably compensated for time spent, that copying costs be reimbursed, or that an individual's identity be concealed. Courts may also issue protective orders relating to the production of requested documents.

In light of the broad discretion afforded to district courts by § 1782, appellate review of orders made pursuant to the statute is extremely deferential, inquiring only as to whether the court erred in its interpretation of the language of the statute and, if not, whether the decision to provide assistance constituted an abuse of discretion.

Applicability of Federal Rules of Civil Procedure

Section 1782(a) provides that the order may require in whole or in part that the practice and procedure of the foreign country be followed but "[t]o the extent . . . the order does not prescribe otherwise, the testimony or statement shall be taken, and the document or other thing produced, in accordance with the Federal Rules of Civil Procedure." This provides flexibility to the party seeking discovery to request procedures tailored to the requirements of the jurisdiction in which the testimony or other evidence is to be used.

Voluntary Discovery

Finally, § 1782(b) contemplates that "a person within the United States" may voluntarily provide testimony or documentary evidence for use in a proceeding in a foreign or international tribunal. Where this is the case, an application for assistance under § 1782(a) is unnecessary.

Section 1782(b) does not specify the procedures to be used when attempting to gather evidence voluntarily, but simply provides that testimony or documentary evidence may be produced in any acceptable manner. Where the party seeking discovery has invoked the district court's authority under § 1782(a), the Federal Rules will likely apply even if some of that evidence is arguably provided voluntarily. In the absence of court intervention under § 1782(a), a party seeking voluntary discovery should consider the law of the foreign jurisdiction in order to ensure that appropriate procedures are followed in gathering the evidence, and that any evidence produced is in admissible form.

28 U.S.C.S. § 1783 — Subpoena of person in foreign country

(a) A court of the United States may order the issuance of a subpoena requiring the appearance as a witness before it, or before a person or body designated by it, of a national or resident of the United States who is in a foreign country, or requiring the production of a specified document or other thing by him, if the court finds that particular testimony or the production of the document or other thing by him is necessary in the interest of justice, and, in other than a criminal action or proceeding, if the court finds, in addition, that it is not possible to obtain his testimony in admissible form without his personal appearance or to obtain the production of the document or other thing in any other manner.

(b) The subpoena shall designate the time and place for the appearance or for the production of the document or other thing. Service of the subpoena and any order to show cause, rule, judgment, or decree authorized by this section or by section 1784 of this title shall be effected in accordance with the provisions of the Federal Rules of Civil Procedure relating to service of process on a person in a foreign country. The person serving the subpoena shall tender to the person to whom the subpoena is addressed his estimated necessary travel and attendance expenses, the amount of which shall be determined by the court and stated in the order directing the issuance of the subpoena.

Commentary

Janis M. Meyer
Dewey Ballantine LLP

28 USCS § 1783 is a rarely invoked provision that empowers federal courts to issue subpoenas on United States residents or nationals who are in a foreign country. The subpoena can require persons to produce documents or other things or to appear before the court or another designated place for testimony. In *Blackmer v. United States*, 284 U.S. 421, 76 L. Ed. 375, 52 S. Ct. 252 (1932), the Supreme Court sanctioned Congress's sovereign authority to recall its citizens and residents to complete certain civic duties, such as assisting the administration of justice. The Court

wrote, "it [cannot] be doubted that the United States possesses the power inherent in sovereignty to require the return to this country of a citizen, resident elsewhere, whenever the public interest requires it, and to penalize him in case of refusal."

The statute is applicable only to U.S. citizens and residents, and subpoenas served on a non-resident alien abroad are void. See *United States v. Farfan-Carreon* 935 F.2d 678 (5th Cir. Tex. 1991).

This power is therefore somewhat analogous to an exercise of long-arm jurisdiction in that citizenship and residency may constitute "minimum contacts" with the United States, and thus it is not unfair to ask citizens and residents to return to this country to testify.

Requirements for Issuance of a § 1783 Subpoena

Section 1783 establishes separate criteria for obtaining a subpoena in criminal and civil cases. A § 1783 subpoena is available in all criminal proceedings, including grand jury proceedings, provided the testimony or other evidence is necessary "in the interest of justice."

In civil matters, however, a party must show not only that the witness's testimony, documents, or things are necessary "in the interest of justice" but also that the evidence cannot be obtained in any other admissible form. This analysis requires a balancing of the need for the testimony against the burden on the witness. As Sen. Rep. No. 1580 (1964), *reprinted in* USCCAN 3782, 3791, states:

> In determining whether the issuance of a [subpoena] is in the interest of justice, the court may take into account the nature of the proceedings, the nature of the testimony or the evidence sought, the convenience of the witness or the producer of the evidence, the convenience of the parties, and other facts bearing upon the reasonableness of requiring a person abroad to appear as a witness or to produce tangible evidence. [These] criteria guarantee not only that in proper cases a [subpoena] will always be available, but

also that burdens upon U.S. citizens and residents abroad will not be imposed without compelling reason.

The party seeking the evidence must therefore show that the testimony cannot be obtained by, for example, the voluntary return of the witness to the United States or the use of deposition testimony obtained through international legal assistance measures that do not require the return of the witness to the U.S. See 28 USCS § 1781.

This raises an interesting dilemma for the litigant seeking a § 1783 subpoena. If the witness has given or can give out-of-court testimony such testimony is admissible only if the witness is deemed unavailable under Rule 804(a) of the Federal Rules of Evidence. The factors considered for determining whether a witness is unavailable under Rule 804(a) are similar to those considered under § 1783 to determine whether testimony cannot be obtained in admissible form by other means. This could lead to an unintended result.

The argument that a §1783 subpoena is needed because the witness will not voluntarily return to this country also supports the position that out-of-court testimony obtained pursuant to international legal assistance measures will be admissible because the witness is unavailable within the meaning of FRE 804(a). This would render a §1783 subpoena unwarranted because admissible testimony can be obtained by other means. This may be one reason for the infrequent issuance of §1783 subpoenas.

Procedures under § 1783

Section 1783(b) provides that the subpoena shall designate the time and place of appearance or for production and may be served in accordance with the Federal Rules of Civil Procedure pertaining to service of process on a person in a foreign country. The court shall also determine the estimated costs associated with answering the subpoena (travel and attendant expenses, etc.) and include that figure in the subpoena itself. This sum shall then be tendered to the person when served.

The FRCP provide that service of process upon individuals in a foreign country may be made by any internationally agreed means reasonably calculated to give notice, in any manner acceptable under the service of process rules of the foreign state or by personal or postal delivery or any other means not prohibited by the law or rules of the foreign state. See FRCP 4(f).

As is the case with other procedures for serving process or obtaining evidence abroad, it is prudent to seek the advice of counsel in the jurisdiction in which the witness is located prior to issuance of the subpoena. Although the subpoena is directed at a U.S. citizen or resident, many foreign states consider the taking of evidence to be a judicial function and a § 1783 subpoena may be considered an infringement on the foreign state's sovereignty.

These jurisdictions, moreover, often desire to preserve their rules and privileges while protecting from undue coercion persons within their jurisdiction, whether or not they are nationals. Thus, local counsel in the jurisdiction in which the witness resides can advise as to whether service should be made pursuant to the Convention on the Service Abroad of Judicial and Extra-Judicial Documents in Civil or Commercial Matters, 20 U.S.T. 361, 1969 U.S.T. LEXIS 152, or other means of international legal assistance and whether there are any legal procedures to be followed to ensure that the proposed witness will not be able successfully to challenge the subpoena in the foreign jurisdiction.

Enforcement of § 1783

Failure to appear or produce as ordered under § 1783 is punishable as contempt pursuant to the procedures set forth in 28 USCS § 1784.